A Father's Day Gift

Lifetime Adventures and Hidden Gems

Jason George

Published by Jason George

Goleta, CA

Hardback ISBN: 978-1-7351979-2-0
Paperback ISBN: 978-1-7351979-1-3
Ebook ISBN: 978-1-7351979-0-6

Cover Art Copyright © 2020 Fiona Jayde Media
Interior design by Tamara Cribley, The Deliberate Page
Editing by Chris Knight, The Deliberate Page

Contents

Introduction

There are three things that I love: God, the outdoors, and my family. I have always wanted to be a dad and I am blessed to call MD and Andrew (aka Smiley Andy) my sons. For me, being a dad has been a lifelong process of learning how to teach, guide, and raise my sons in a way so that when they become adults they are equipped with the right tools so they may live their lives to the fullest. I'm learning from my children as much as I am teaching them, which has been challenging and humbling. As I learn these lessons on how to better my parenting I thank the Lord for His grace and mercy and for giving me many chances to keep trying.

This book is dedicated to my father, Eric George. He invested in my life by simply spending time with me and sharing his passions with me. I have fond memories like playing catch with a football at night under the moon in the street, all the soccer games he coached for me, and summers in the Santa Ynez river swimming and catching crawdads. He was a busy man and sometimes our time together was simply me riding along in his Deputy Sheriff car during his shift. My dad had a Cal-30 sailboat named Vuelo, which means flight. We sailed on it a lot. He tried to teach me sailing to hand over the tiller, so to speak, but I wasn't interested. Growing up, we spent a lot of time on golf courses together, one of his favorite pastimes. I still use the same putter he bought me as a kid. I cannot get rid of it, because it reminds me of all the times we played golf together. A very special bonding time was us driving together from California to Colorado where I was first attending Colorado Christian University. As far as camping is concerned, my dad and I actually only went camping together once, riding horseback into the mountains and having fun camping for several days, but we had to hike the entire way back and he still reminds me to this day that I complained the whole way. I recall wondering, where did the horses go?

I find peace and strength in the outdoors; hiking and camping and relaxing and playing in the wilderness are exercises I use to tune out from my daily grind and ground myself with God and in nature. This is such an important aspect of my life, I couldn't wait to start sharing it with my sons. You'll note that my first adventure documented here is with MD when he was four years old. Some might balk at his young age, but children are adaptable and I would never lead my sons into harm's way. Instead, we go on adventures together, learn about ourselves and each other together, and about God's love. This shared love of the outdoors has brought us closer than any other activity we have done. The results have been deep and meaningful conversations, support and encouragement, visible growth and maturity of my sons, and the expression of love for one another.

I hope my documentation of these experiences together inspires you. You can make an impact on a child's life and experience the joy one receives when you have invested in that child. I feel humbled and blessed to be a dad; to raise them, teach them, love and forgive them, restore and comfort them, build them up and let them go when they become men to hopefully become dads themselves. I sometimes laugh that God has given me, such an imperfect dad as myself, these two boys. And this is our journey together, the three of us, to learn and grow in His name.

Special Thanks

I want to say a special thanks to my beautiful and precious bride, Melody, who entrusted me to take our sons on these sometimes wild adventures. I appreciate that although she doesn't go on our trips, she helps by setting us up with groceries, making cookies and brownies, and doing our dishes when we come home. She tucks sweet notes into my backpack or gear bag that I read while I'm away. She allows me to buy all our specialized gear which is an investment and I will pass it down to the boys as they grow older. I am so grateful for her prayers too as God has watched over us.

I also want to say thank you to my friends and family, my mom Linda and sister Stephanie, for encouraging me to sit and write all these stories. I especially want to say thank you to my biggest cheerleader, Peggy Kahler, who not only encouraged and inspired but challenged me to write this book. It's been a joy to put these pieces together to create a book so others might read it and be inspired. I need to especially recognize her financial support through God's grace and provision.

These adventures in the outdoors would not have been possible if it were not for my college buddy at Colorado Christian University. His name is Cullen Purser. At age nineteen he started making and sewing his own sleeping bags and backpacks. He took me on my first overnight winter backpacking trip in the local Colorado mountains outside Lakewood. We hiked in several miles through the snow in a beautiful forest of aspen trees, camped in my cheap three-season tent (which I still have for the kids to play in), ate Top Ramen for dinner, slept in my new Wiggy's sleeping bag with a one-inch sleeping pad and froze the whole night and thawed out by the time I got home. I was hooked and never looked back. I truly thank him for showing me this passion for the outdoors, especially winter backpacking. He is amazing! He currently handmakes caravan trailers with his brothers at their business, Vintage Overland, in Grand Junction, CO. He is so gifted and extremely humble.

Thank you to all who have joined me on my trips. I appreciate your friendship which has grown because of these adventures. I hope these are just the beginning for you as you continue to embrace life and explore what God has created before you.

Finally, I thank my God, my Lord and Savior, Jesus Christ, for giving me such a wonderful family, Melody, MD, and Andrew, and to be able to take my kids on these adventures. He has always kept us safe, blessed us with great weather, and provided resources when we needed them most. He has brought me and my sons closer together because of His spectacular creation that we enjoy exploring. He has brought me and my sister closer together as well. He has sparked a flame in others to come and explore with me that which He has created. I have built lifetime friendships along the way on these adventures. Thank you so much, God.

1st Backpacking Trip with MD

Figueroa Mountain, June 7-8, 2010

I decided to take MD (age four) on our first backpacking trip together up Figueroa Mountain. It's a short drive and I knew MD would be able to handle the hike with lots of my encouragement. At this age, he was always looking for an adventure and was climbing trees and playing sports. I figured that backpacking would just be a new challenge for him, and he'd either love it or hate it, but I wanted to give him a chance. I was really looking forward to this new bonding experience with him.

This area is local to us, and I have hiked it before, but it had been a long time since I'd been there, so I needed a little extra time to find the trailhead and park. We loaded our packs onto our backs and started to walk. We took this two-mile hike slowly, and I gave MD a lot of encouragement; frequently saying "Hang in there, son." There were lots of switchbacks and narrow spots so I really had my eye on him. He complained a little bit that he was tired, and it was a hot day which made hiking harder, but he kept going. I decided we would head far enough up the trail to be away from the road and day hikers, and we found a great spot right next to the creek. There was quite a bit of poison oak growing nearby, so I gave MD a long lecture to stay away from it and not touch it. My father-in-law had made it very clear to me that MD was to come back home safely in one piece—he never mentioned my safety, it was all about his grandson.

After arriving and checking out the spot a bit more, a hiker passed through, and we exchanged pleasant and kind words before he continued. But just forty-five minutes later he was back, asking me for a jump start for the dead battery in his car. I wanted to help him, but we had just arrived after our long hike. I told him about an RV I'd seen parked down the road that might be able to help, and he set off. Unbelievably about an hour later this poor guy was back, saying he hadn't found anyone. I felt terrible and guilty for the trouble I had made for him, so I offered him my car keys. I told him to use my car for the jump start and then leave the keys hidden in the fender in the wheel well.

Since the afternoon had gotten hot, I encouraged MD to play in the water in the creek while I set up the tent that our friend Matt Doty had loaned us. When I finished, I joined MD in the water to cool off but right as I stepped in, a two-and-a-half-foot long gopher snake swam right past my waist. Rather than jumping away, I grabbed it and took it to the nearby bushes to release it. Thank the Lord it did not come near MD or bite him. After a few hours playing in the water, MD and I came back to our campsite. We put the rain fly on the tent together, I showed him how to store our food high up in a tree to keep it safe from critters and how to build a fire, where we cooked a dinner of tri-tip and rice. We had a wonderful evening and soon fell quickly to sleep.

The next morning we woke up, had pancakes for breakfast, and headed back into the water. We hiked up the creek as far as we could go and had a lot of fun. When we returned to camp, we packed up our gear and hiked back out to our car.

MD hung in there during our hike out. We made it back to the car and found the keys in the fender as I'd asked—plus a kind note from the stranded hiker we'd helped. We drove home at the end of this hike that was hopefully the beginning of a life-long journey for me and my son.

Attempt West Lion Canyon Falls & Rose Valley Falls

June 16, 2011

MD and I talked about our first trip quite often over the past year. He'd had a fun time and was looking forward to going out again. I spent some time researching a new spot for us and talked with a local park ranger. I had a couple of spots in mind and we drove to the Lion Canyon Falls area in the mountains of Ojai, California. Melody stayed home with little Andrew and again my father-in-law made a point of reminding me to keep MD safe.

A large part of why I do these trips with my sons is to share an important part of my spiritual life with them. I find myself closest to God when I am in the mountains, surrounded by peace, nature, and quiet, and far from the distractions of everyday life. While I hike and camp in nature I feel like my reset button is pushed and I can return to the daily grind with fresh eyes and an open mind. I use it as a time to surrender that which is keeping me from growing in the Lord. Being up in the mountains is powerful; Moses, of the Old Testament of the Bible, hiked up Mt. Sinai so he could meet God and receive His Ten Commandments. I, too, have used my hiking trips to pray and be closer to the Lord. Like Jesus Christ, he wandered in the wilderness for forty days, praying and fasting while he was being tempted by Satan, and afterward began his ministry before his eventual death and resurrection. Once, I even climbed a mountain to pray for God's wisdom and confirmation as I was preparing to ask Melody to be my wife.

We started our hike on Lion Canyon Falls Trail, but the trail was so full of poison oak we had to use the creek instead. We hiked for three-quarters of a mile until we found a tiny spot and camped there overnight even though there was so much poison oak. We tried going up the creek further, but we didn't reach the falls. This was a great lesson for MD and me; sometimes we might not reach our destination as planned, but we should always make use of what we have in front of us. We had a great time, made a wonderful dinner meal together, and laughed and played in the refreshing creek next to our campsite. When we woke up the next morning, my son was cuddled up next to me. It was the best feeling. I did not care where we were. This is all I needed. Being with my son, in my arms, sleeping peacefully and content. At that moment, I thought to myself, I love being his dad.

The next morning we talked about what we should do. We could stay here or try to go up the creek further, but instead, we retreated down the creek, got back in the car, and drove to Rose Valley Falls just ten minutes away. There were campsites near where we had parked, but I wanted to camp right at Rose Valley Falls. We did a short hike which took less than fifteen minutes and set up a camp just big enough for our tent next to the waterfall. This was a great spot! It was so awesome. We met lots of people who were hiking through to see the waterfall. I started to feel a little bit awkward as more and more people came to see the waterfall because I felt I was infringing on their space. Looking back, we probably should have not camped there, but it was so cool to have done it, and I am so glad we did. We had lots of fun. MD and I tried our best to hike up to another massive waterfall, but it was too steep, and the rocks were too unsteady for us. So, we stayed at "our" waterfall instead, and played in it and explored the cave behind the waterfall during the day.

During the late afternoon, a woman and her dog came to enjoy the beautiful waterfall and we found out by talking with her that she had been on the *Survivor* television show two seasons prior. Her name is Alina Wilson and she had a few great stories about that experience, and afterward, every year she has made a commitment to take a journey with her dog somewhere for the amount of time she stayed on the Survivor show.

I really enjoyed the whole package of this trip. We faced some challenges, like shortening our hike to West Fork Lion Canyon Falls but making the best out of it. We learned the lesson that sometimes the journey we are on takes a turn and we have to improvise, make adjustments, accept change, and embrace it all. We were blessed by an incredible waterfall and got to meet Alina Wilson from *Survivor*. Ultimately, MD and I had a blast, just the two of us, and that connection was exactly what we needed this time.

Dad, MD, & Our Buddy Ryan Corum

"You're Never Too Young to Start"

Sierra Backpacking/Snowshoeing, January 14, 2012

Ryan and I first met while working together at Mount Hermon Christian Camps in Santa Cruz, California. I was the climbing wall director and he was one of my staff, but we became close friends outside of work responsibilities. We even climbed up a platform on the ropes course and slept in our sleeping bags with our harnesses secured to the redwood tree. We went on many climbing trips and winter backpacking trips by cross country skiing. He now works for Search and Rescue for the Visalia Sheriff's Department. He loves to have fun and is very funny, so MD connected with him immediately and easily.

Speaking of MD, my son was not yet six years old when I decided it was a great time to take him winter camping. At just five years, seven months, again my protective father-in-law made a point to remind me to keep MD, his grandson, safe—Melody was fine with the trip, as always. Her trust in me is uplifting and supportive.

On a side note, winter camping presents a few obvious challenges. Being cold is miserable, but it can become unsafe and even life-threatening if the conditions go bad. There is plenty of good equipment available, though, and I've spent more time and money doing my research and working with different backpacking companies to ensure my gear is the best. Most companies want to work with you; they want to help and inspire you and your kids to get out and have a fun adventure.

To give you an idea of what is required for winter backpacking in the snow, I'll explain my gear. I have a Mountain Hardwear four-season tent designed to handle harsh elements, which is a smart shelter to have. I use an insulated sleeping pad by Nemo as a barrier between me and the ground, which keeps cold air from penetrating my sleeping bag. It has a built-in foot pump so you do not have to stress your lungs by blowing up your pad in high altitude conditions and trapping moisture from your breath inside the pad, rendering it possibly useless. A sleeping pad can make or break your sleeping experience and possibly your entire trip experience. My down sleeping bag, made by Mountain Hardwear, is rated -20 degrees for winter trips. This type of bag is lightweight, compressible, waterproof, and really keeps you warm. My winter clothing includes a jacket and pants that are waterproof, windproof, and breathable. I wear a base layer and a down jacket. And, of course, wool-like socks, winter boots, and warm gloves. Now you are ready for a winter adventure.

For our first winter camping trip, MD and I headed to the Sierra Mountains. We drove to Visalia to stay overnight with Ryan and his wife in their home. MD had a headache all day during our drive up and then at 2300 hours he vomited the beef jerky he'd eaten during our road trip. I have never eaten beef jerky again because of that night! In the morning, MD said he was feeling well enough to go, so we did. We drove up near Huntington Lake, parked on the side of the road, and hiked the Tamarack Trail two miles in.

During our three days at camp, we had a lot of small adventures. Ryan only stayed one night with us, but he and MD had a lot of fun together those first two days. We didn't have much snow and the streams and meadows were mostly frozen. I taught MD how to filter water from the semi-frozen stream from my MSR HyperFlow purifier, we collected firewood, and sledded over frozen meadows which was a blast for MD. We even saw a fish swimming under the ice, but it was too hard to catch. We did some snowshoeing and hung out together in our tent. We ate well and enjoyed our favorites of tri-tip and pancakes.

The second night was cold, really cold, getting down to only 5-10 degrees. There was frost on the ground in the morning, and it was still a bone-chilling 15 degrees at 0900 hours. We tried some hand warmers, but after thirty minutes they were ineffective, and MD made good use of them by playing games inside the tent. The sun finally came up and warmed us just enough to get going and head back to the car.

During our hike back, MD got a headache again, and his fingers were cold. I think he didn't drink enough water. Where the trail had ice (about 65% of our hike), I could pull him behind me on our saucer. MD was getting more exhausted and the headache was not going away. So, at one point for about 1/8th of a mile, I ended up carrying my backpack, his backpack, and MD on my shoulders, while hauling our trekking poles and snowshoes. I think I burned two thousand calories on the hike back, though it was only two miles.

Our first winter trip was a harder one for MD, and I was proud that he handled it all. He'd had two headaches and gotten sick to his stomach but still managed all the necessities of base camp and stayed safe. The added bonus was seeing Ryan again, introducing him to MD, and having mountain time with clear minds to continue to strengthen our friendship and fellowship.

Backpacking Trip to West Lion Canyon Falls & East Lion Canyon Falls

July 7, 2012

MD and I decided to go back to the Lion Canyon Falls in the upper mountains of Ojai where we'd tried an attempt the previous year. Again, the trail was overgrown with poison oak, and again we hiked in the dry creek bed, but this time we continued and didn't turn back. MD was six years old and had persevered through the winter challenge, and I hoped he'd remember this location as a fun spot to encourage him through a tough hike.

It was 103 degrees during the day while we were up there. We found one pond along the way that was only three feet long and maybe four inches deep, but there were three trout in it. One was already dead. We caught a live one by hand, it was about ten inches long, and we put it back in. When we came by this pond two days later, the fish were gone as was the water. All that was left was mud.

We camped for two nights. It took us three and a quarter hours to get to the West Lion Canyon Falls, where we set up our base camp. We explored the surrounding area and found the creek with some intermittent water holes. I showed MD again how to use the water filter so that we could stock up on clean, purified water. It was very hot and we needed to stay hydrated. We also tried fishing for the first time. MD didn't catch any fish, but he captured my heart! We ate our traditional tri-tip dinner, then we headed for bed.

The next day, we hiked up the dry creek bed until we came to the place where there were supposed to be waterfalls but they were all dried up. It was kind of sad and disappointing. We were so hot and just wanted to cool off and play in the water.

We decided to hike to East Lion Canyon Falls. It took us about an hour to get there. We followed the trail markers along the way, but at times, we were not sure where the trail was leading us. It was scorching hot. We took our shirts, soaked them with water from our water bottles, and wrapped them around our heads to keep us cool. I am so thankful MD filtered lots of water because we sure needed it. Once we got to the East Lion Canyon Falls, there were pockets of water about three to four feet deep. It was not the cleanest water, but we were overheating and needed to cool off. So, we did. After several hours there, we had lunch, rehydrated, and headed back to base camp.

We ate spaghetti for dinner and then tried to fish again, but no nibbles on the bait. We went to bed under the stars. It was so beautiful. I was so thankful to be here with my son. It was a good day, despite the heat and lack of waterfalls.

The next morning, we had breakfast and headed back to our car. We wanted an early start since it was so hot during the day and there was very little water down the creek bed. We did a lot of boulder hopping along the way. There were a couple of times we could use the trail but then it closed in on us with poison oak so we went back on the dry creek bed.

The conditions during this trip were ruthless, but we survived. MD was amazing and did exceptionally well, and I'm so proud of him.

40-Mile Bike Trek to Carpinteria

July 2012

When MD was just three years old, he learned how to ride a bike. When he was four, he rode 11.55 miles with me. He would ride a tiny, 14" wheel bike with his feet spinning around on the crank to stay up with me. By the age of six, he and I were cycling a lot. We trained for months for this trip, riding ten miles, two to three days a week. We did one 25-mile ride and he did great. For this adventure, we upgraded him to a 24", 21-speed mountain bike. It was huge on him but he needed the gear ratio and bigger wheels.

We decided to ride our bikes from Goleta, California, to Carpinteria which is about 40 miles away. We left on a Friday morning, waving our arms to mommy and baby Andrew, saying goodbye and how we'd see them in two days. We rode to the Mesa in Santa Barbara, had lunch with my father-in-law, played at two parks, and then headed to the breakwater at the Harbor. Taking frequent breaks helped a lot to keep our momentum going. Riding with a child takes longer and can be very tiring, so breaks are good for both of us. We had great conversations along the way. We then rode back up to the Mesa and camped overnight in the backyard of a friend's house. They even had a putting green in the backyard, so we got to play with that as well.

The next morning, we went out to breakfast with my mom and niece. It was a great opportunity to spend time with them and enjoy yummy food. We rode to the Santa Barbara Zoo and met up with Melody, baby Smiley Andy, and my mother-in-law, Margaret. We spent the afternoon there seeing all the animals.

After that, MD and I rode to Carpinteria, the last stretch of our bike trek. I continued to cheer MD along the way, encourage him, and motivate him as his little legs were getting tired and his butt was sore—so was mine. When we arrived, I was so excited and cheered on MD for his great accomplishment. I thought he would crash and want to sleep because I sure did. We played at the State Beach for a while and then went to another friend's house and set up camp in their backyard. From there we went out to dinner and then watched a movie on an inflatable screen on the State Park lawn.

The next day, we went to the best breakfast in the area—Esau's Restaurant in Carpinteria. After our bellies were full, we needed spiritual food. We rode our bikes to the First Baptist Church where my friend, Joe Epley is the pastor. Joe Epley was my pastor at the church in Santa Barbara while I was growing up and he made a huge impact in my life.

After that, MD and I played down at the beach and then waited for the train. We took the Amtrak train back to Goleta where we were greeted by Melody and Smiley Andy at the train station. MD and I got back on our bikes and we rode home. It was about 40 miles over the three days, the bulk of it on the first two days. It was a blast. So much fun, and a great bonding time with my son. I was so impressed with MD's endurance, confidence on the bike, positive attitude, and willingness to take on this challenge at such a young age—just six years old. We want to do it again after our rubbery legs get back to normal.

Dad, MD, Ben, & Mason Sierra Trip

"A Snowman, A Snow Cave, and Snow Much Fun"

February 15, 2013

MD and I went on a four-day winter backpacking trip requiring snowshoes with two other buddies, Ben Parker and Mason Parker (not related). There was a lot of snow this winter season. We drove up early in the morning to Huntington Lake and parked at the Tamarack Lodge. Melody made brownies for me to give to the owner, Gere, and his wife, Mary Lou, in exchange for parking there.

We hiked five and a half miles in by snowshoes all morning and afternoon. It was such a long day. MD needed lots of encouragement as he snowshoed slowly up the trail. We finally made it to base camp, set up our tent, and started cooking our favorite dinner of tri-tip, beans, and rice. It was late by then and we used headlamps to cook our food. MD, Mason, and I slept in our tent while Ben slept outside with his new Nemo Cosmo Insulated sleeping pad and new Mountain Hardwear Wraith sleeping bag on a tarp under the clear, dark, starry skies.

The next morning, I made breakfast of eggs and sausage with hot chocolate to warm our cold bodies. Today, we needed to make our campsite a livable one. The guys and I spent the second day making our living conditions as sweet as possible. We made a trench that was 45 feet long, three feet wide, and three and a half feet deep. At one end was the kitchen area and at the other end were the two bedrooms—snow caves, one for Ben, and one for Mason, MD and me in another. It was awesome. At one point in the day some snowmobilers passed by, but out of curiosity turned around and wanted a tour of our living quarters. They were amazed. One of the snowmobilers was named Mayor Mark, who later in my life became a friend.

We slept in a snow cave, a bit tight. MD kept waking up and trying to sit up, but I had to brace his head from hitting the ceiling of the snow cave. Those several nights in the snow cave were a little rough.

This was an incredible trip for all of us. During our adventure there, we made a snowman, played in the snow, climbed trees to get a better view of the mountains, and relaxed. We ate really well. We all bonded and my son became very close to these men who later have become a positive role model for both my kids. It was one of the best trips so far. I did have one challenging moment when MD had a meltdown and I placed him in a time-out sitting under a tree. He later apologized to the three of us all for his behavior. It was one of those moments where being a parent is hard. Ben and Mason were so gracious, forgiving, and supportive.

On the way back, the guys pulled MD on a round sled almost all the way back to our car. He really enjoyed that. On the drive home, we stopped in Kettleman City to eat at In-N-Out. That was some tasty food after a long backpacking trip.

On a side note, Ben Parker's wife, Emily, wrote a wonderful article in our local Santa Barbara News-Press that was published on the day we left which detailed our winter trip last year and what was to come.

Who Is Mason Parker?

On our last winter backpacking trip, Mason joined us. I want to share with you how we met and the impact he has made on my whole family. Mason is like family; he is family to us George's.

I met Mason for the first time at a Multi-Sport Ministry (a Christian-based sports ministry for athletes who compete in triathlons and other races) at my house with four other guys. Out of all the guys, I thought he would be the least likely for me to get to know. He was very quiet and distant. About a year later we reconnected while he was working at Santa Barbara Running. He was a big runner and interested in triathlons. So, being that I was a triathlete, I trained him to become a triathlete and our friendship grew really fast. He would call me "gramps" since he was much younger—I graduated from high school the same year when he was born, in 1990. He soon became part of my family and bonded immediately with my sons and grew attached to them. We competed together in the Santa Barbara Triathlon, his first race. So to prepare him, I gave him a care package to help him with his race day. The package included baby formula for a pre-race meal, a diaper to keep the ocean clean during his swim, and later a rubber ducky in his water bucket in the Transition Area while he rinsed his feet after the ocean swim. He still carries the rubber ducky in his race bag to this day and it has been over ten years. I also gave him baby powder to help him freshen up after the race to meet the girls. He wrote me a card in crayon and he titled it, "To: Grandpa Jason." The letters R, N, and S were written backwards. He wrote, "You have really made this summer the best one I have ever had. You have helped me grow into more of a man. Thank you so much for spending all the time you did with me. I love you, Jason. Your Training Partner, Mason Parker. P.S. Your hospitality has been second to none. And Mel, thanks for letting me train with Jason even though I made him late so often."

Mason has also been my right hand man on so many winter trips. He knows how I think and operate. He is very conscientious, safe, and a very hard worker. His presence makes it even more enjoyable on the trips. He is so good with my kids on the trips, too. One trip, just him and I, we made a snow cave 7' x 7' x 6' with 15 stairs leading down to the snow cave. Mason put up a sign on the inside of the snow cave, "Our Home" with twigs. It was awesome! He is a blast to hang out with. Thank you, Mason, for being in my life and part of my family. I love you as a brother and as a "grandson."

Dad, MD, & Smiley Andy Rattlesnake Canyon Trip

"Did you say rattlesnake?"

March 27, 2013

This would be the first trip together for me with both MD and Smiley Andy. I was not sure if the two boys would be too much for me to handle. Taking one son meant a lot of planning and responsibility. But, we also got great one-on-one time. Taking two kids is a bit more of a challenge. More gear, having my attention wrestled between two sons, and keeping them both safe. In the end, I decided to test my fatherhood skills and my backpacking skills together, and I hoped to have a good outcome and enjoy the process.

I took them up Rattlesnake Canyon Trail about one and a half miles into our local mountains during the afternoon. MD carried his pack all the way there and back. Andrew, almost three years old, hiked about 1.2 miles until I carried him. It was evening when we found a sweet little camping area nestled within the trees next to the creek. We set up camp and hung out. Hikers would pass by, say hi and tell us that it was a really cool spot to camp. I shared with them that this was my first camping trip with both kids and wanted something close to home if something went wrong. It was a huge responsibility to manage it all for two small children.

We had fun. The boys got along most of the time. Andrew pouted for a while, but then smiled and life was just fine. We had spaghetti for dinner and crawled into bed. The next morning, we ate pancakes and then packed up. On the way back, I mostly carried Andrew. It was a quick overnight trip.

MD was a big help with cooking and watching over Andrew. It was a bit stressful with a little one and I do not think I relaxed except when I was in the tent sleeping. He really wanted to go home the next morning, so we did.

I hope this is one of many trips that I will do with my kids together. For now, I think I will take one son at a time unless I have a friend that comes along. I strongly believe that going on these adventures with my boys will create a deeper relationship with them. I love them and want them to experience life to the fullest within safe guidelines.

MD, Andrew, & Dad 60-Mile Bike Trek

"Broken Arms and Broken Hearts"

July 17, 2013

The boys and I planned a sixty-mile ride to Carpinteria State Beach and home again over three days. It was a year ago that MD and I rode down together and took the train back to Goleta and with all our training I decided we could do this long ride. MD (seven years old) rode his own bike and I had Andrew (three years old) in the

Co-Pilot seat behind me while pulling a Burley bike trailer with all our gear.

To work ourselves into shape, MD and I started doing more frequent rides of ten to twelve miles and also started riding to church and home on Sundays; an 18-mile trip with hills to further help strengthen us. A 60-mile ride is long even for an adult! I didn't include any longer rides during our training, as we never had a large enough window of time free. I knew if we could do about ten miles and then take a break we'd be ready for a long day of riding with breaks.

The other part of this adventure would be me having both boys. That's not just an additional child to watch and care for, I'd also have the additional gear to haul and set up. The energy spent with both kids is split up and that can become challenging when one child wants or needs more attention for whatever reason. On the other hand, the older child can be a help with either setting up or watching the younger sibling, or they can play together and stay mutually occupied while the adult can do some work.

The State Beach at Carpinteria is great for kids and families. The boys love to play at the beach, in the ocean, and on the playground there, and they were really excited about this trip. Camping together would be great too, as well as cooking our own steaks to order at The Palms Restaurant. The three of us wanted the time outdoors.

We started off from home in Goleta and rode to Summerland where we stopped to take a break and have playtime. I had my back turned for just a moment so I didn't see exactly what happened, but Andrew either pushed or kicked Matthew off the top of a play structure. Matthew fell approximately six feet backward. He had cuts and abrasions on his face and leg and was in a lot of pain, and I was pretty sure both of his arms were broken. He had been wearing his bike helmet. While the visor was cracked, he didn't seem to have a concussion. I called Melody at work and told her what had happened. She rushed home, switched cars, and drove down to Summerland to pick us up. She was tied up with traffic, taking two hours to get to us which should have been a thirty-minute drive.

While we were waiting, I continued to check on MD. A couple of women had seen what had happened and brought over a couple of ice packs (which we still have today). Paramedics who I knew from work were parked nearby, so I was able to get some supplies from them. It became clear to me that if MD hadn't been wearing his helmet he could've suffered life-threatening injuries.

Andrew knew I was very angry with him. He would not enter a ten-foot perimeter around me as I was caring for MD. He knew that what he did was wrong, but I wasn't sure he grasped the extent of the situation. Looking back now, I'm not sure if he was of an age to understand guilt or that the situation was scary for MD and me. He did know that I was upset and very concerned about his brother's condition. Afterward, at home, I reiterated the importance of safety, respect, and kindness. To not forget that they are brothers and although it is in their genes to be annoying and irritating to each other, that physical confrontation is never acceptable. I emphasized how MD showed grace, love, forgiveness, and even concern for us continuing our trip without him, while he was suffering in pain and disappointment.

Once Melody reached us, we went straight to the emergency department at the Goleta Valley hospital and had x-rays done. MD had a fracture in each wrist, not breaks through the entire bone, but he would need casts done by an orthopedist. The ER sent us home with both MD's arms in splints in less than two hours.

MD's attitude was awesome through the whole ordeal. The x-ray techs told us he was the best patient they'd had all day. While he was lying on the grass at the Summerland Park in immense pain, he told me that he loved his brother and that he wanted me and Andrew to continue on our trip without him. What a brave and loving kid. He makes me very proud, and we were so grateful for how strong, calm, and courteous he remained through it all.

Our friends and family rallied for MD over the weekend. My wife and I notified our close relatives and people from our church to be praying for us. This was a traumatic experience and really scared us, and their prayers bathed him in rest and provision—we were able to see an orthopedist on Monday to get him into casts. God was really watching over us so very closely.

I love my two boys so much. I can't wait to redo this trip—without any play structures.

MD & Dad Backpacking to Del Norte Campsite, Santa Cruz Island

"Water Rationing but Surrounded by Water"

August 3-5, 2013

MD and I went backpacking for three days on Santa Cruz Island, which is part of the nearby Channel Islands. We left on Saturday by boat from Ventura and landed at Prisoners Harbor, then hiked a grueling ("strenuous" according to the map, which was accurate), 3.5 miles up continuous hills. It took us about two hours and forty-five minutes. It was hot and long. MD gave up his backpack to me about a half of a mile up the trail. For this location, we had to bring our water and food, as there was no water available at camp. So, I ended up carrying eighty pounds on my back, the most I have ever carried, which I hope I never do again.

When we finally made it up to our beautiful campsite, we set up and relaxed. There were four others up there who were really nice and MD in no time made some new friends. One of the locals, a Santa

Cruz fox, spent part of his day hanging out with us. I think the fox liked our company. Of course, we never fed it or touched it even if it was so cute. We ate a dinner of salmon, rice, and veggies and then went to bed by 1800.

The next day we headed off for a "two-mile" hike to Chinese Harbor, at least that is what we were told by a returning hiker. I packed some food and 1.5L of water for a four-mile hike round trip. I told myself that four miles would be do-able. Well, it turned out to be four and a half miles just to get there. MD drank his bottle by the two-and-a-half-mile mark, leaving just one liter for both of us for the next six-and-a-half-miles.

Chinese Harbor was awesome. I snorkeled with a very up close and personal sea lion, which made me a bit nervous. I told the sea lion several times to stay, but he did not listen. Lots of cool stuff to see in the ocean, from sea urchins, starfish, abalone, mussels, clams, jellyfish, crabs, and fish. After several hours there, we headed back up a very steep switchback that seemed endless. Realizing we had only 800mls left of water and it was very hot, we stopped every half-mile to take a drink from the cap of the Nalgene water bottle to make sure we had enough for the hike back. We made it back to camp, 8.78 miles total with one last gulp of water. When we arrived we met two guys, Levi and Jake from Ventura. They were lots of fun and MD had no problems entertaining them with his sense of humor and endless energy (no sugar was given to this boy when we got back). I was pooped, but MD was not! We had spaghetti for dinner and then made our way to our pillows. Before we closed our eyes, we read from God's Word, the Bible, some chapters from 1 John and Proverbs 10 which MD picked out so randomly but they turned out to be appropriate for us. Proverbs 10:1 says, "A wise son makes a glad father, but a foolish son is the grief of his mother." I was a glad father.

Morning came up fast the next day. I woke up at 0600, got out of bed, and walked outside to see the breathtaking sunrise. It was cloudy the morning before so these clear skies were a beautiful change. We joined Levi and Jake for breakfast and shared oatmeal together. It was really enjoyable. The clouds rolled in and we headed back to Prisoners Harbor. MD left ahead of me and he was on a mission. I had complete trust in his navigational skills. I could see him from a distance as he made his way through the switchbacks. I finally caught up with him about twenty minutes later. As we hiked, we talked about how much fun we'd had and all the cool stuff we saw and did. One of the inspiring conversations we had was that when we got back to Ventura we would go to In-N-Out for food and shakes. This was some serious motivation! We arrived at Prisoners ahead of schedule, getting there in just one hour and forty-five minutes. It was 1015 and the boat was not coming until 1500, so we ate our last remaining food and swam in the ocean. MD dared me to jump off the pier but I chickened out. MD said, "Get out of the way, I am going off." And he did just that! He is a tough boy.

Don't forget that he had two broken arms, done just two weeks earlier. I am so proud of my son. He never complained about his casts. He complained a little bit on the trails but so did I. It was really hard. It was so much fun to bond and hang out just the two of us. He is an amazing kid. I am so privileged and blessed to have him as my son.

The boat finally came and we headed back to Ventura and went straight to In-N-Out. We were so hungry. I have never felt this hungry. I felt like I was one of the players on the TV show "Survivor" who wins a reward challenge and the prize is food. It was so good!

Back to normal life and I am very sore. MD went to swim lessons and enjoyed what was left of his summer vacation. It was a fantastic trip and I know that these memories that I build with my two boys will just bring us closer together and build their character, wisdom, and training for the years ahead. Our next trip will be winter backpacking in the Sierras again in January or February. Maybe a 60-mile bike trek before that. We will see.

MD & Dad Winter Sierra Trip

"Lesson: Food is Important"

March 27-29, 2014

This trip was planned to be a four day trip in the Sierras with MD, but somehow I forgot the majority of our food back at home so we cut it short a day. One of my adventure philosophies is that you never know where you're going to end up, and to be as prepared as possible. I'm not only the guide on these trips, but I'm also the planner, the overseer, the Dad, the teacher, the cook, and the sherpa. I suppose I just forgot to put one of those hats on this time.

So, the start of our trip went great. The drive up was smooth that morning as we left really early around 0500. We loaded our packs, although I carried most of the gear. It weighed about 55 pounds. The snowfall this year was pretty good, enough for snowshoes. If you are a parent like me, children can sometimes make the hike in very long. In my case, he was complaining that the backpack was too heavy. For a child this size, fifteen pounds is manageable. After ten minutes into the hike, MD started to complain, saying his back hurt and he was tired. I just kept thinking in my mind, "Try carrying *this* backpack, kid. I am carrying almost all the gear, so stop whining." I decided to unload his pack and I placed it on a saucer that I could drag behind me. When we got to our campsite, we could zip down a hill on the saucer. MD's motivation to hike for miles ended on the first mile where I decided to find a spot to set up camp. It was right near the creek, had lots of snow, was protected by lots of trees, and was off the beaten path. The only sounds we heard were from the creek running by and snow falling off the trees and hitting the ground. So peaceful.

As we set up camp, MD had the idea to "build a snow cave, like Bear Grylls," so we did. We took long branches and sticks and made a teepee-like structure and then placed snow over it to keep it more protected and secure. Well, the weight of the snow caved it in quite a bit so it was very tight and I was not sure if it would be safe to sleep in, and it dripped a lot from the snow on top of the branches which came through the overlay of branches and would get our pad and sleeping bag wet. We tried it anyway and I put in our pads and sleeping bags but MD thought it looked too tight, so we set up the tent for sleeping. We did play in the cave every now and then and MD felt very proud of his work. I shared with him that although it was not a success, it is better to try and fail. We learn from our mistakes and improve our skills so that we can succeed. If you do not try something new, you will never succeed at it. It was a great teaching lesson and a humble moment with my son.

We made a fire to keep ourselves warm and to cook our dinner. I went into the tent in search of our food. I searched everywhere. I went outside to see if I left it there and then back into the tent to rustle through my backpack. I cannot recall how many times I repeated this over and over. I was so frustrated. It seemed like an hour of looking while MD gazed into the fire in a starving hypnotic state. All I found consisted of dehydrated fruit, chicken, tri-tip, and PowerBars. I could not believe it. I made a backpacker's carnal sin, leaving the backpacking food at home. I had never done that before. I am so particular where my stuff is. I found out later when I got home that the food rolled off the table into a bowl which I did not see. Oops! We lived off the food I did bring, and boy, was that tri-tip so good to eat. MD had an idea to fish for a meal so we could stay longer, but we didn't catch anything the next day when we tried. We even looked for grubs to eat off dead wood, nothing to be found. We did decide to cut the trip short and leave a day earlier. We did cook what we had over the coals of our fire and never used my stove and fuel. My inner sherpa just shook his head at me for having to haul the stove and other equipment we never used, but the philosophy is to be prepared.

We made the most of the opportunity. The next morning, we snowshoed about a half or three-quarters of a mile down the creek and then fished. No signs of life in the water to eat. We were hungry for fish. MD claimed he saw a fish, but I think he imagined it. He still claims to this day that he saw one. We continued to explore in both directions and found a huge tree that had fallen across the creek. It must have been 75 feet long. It was massive! We took turns climbing on top of it with our snowshoes for traction because it had snow and ice and stood on top of it as it laid over the creek about twenty feet high above it. It was awesome! In order to cross over the streams, small fallen trees provided a bridge across. MD and I, hand in hand together crossed the creek ever so carefully and slowly. It was a team effort. We were a bit nervous and did not want to fall into the freezing water. We made it safely across, each time we did it realizing we had to depend on each other. It was a trusting moment on each of our parts. At any of those moments crossing the fallen trees, a fall would have been great and I kept thinking how Melody would kill me if either of us got hurt. It was one of those stories I wouldn't want to tell my mom, MD's Nana. I could just hear the lectures from my mom as we crossed in my left ear.

We came back to camp, rehydrated ourselves with refreshing cold water from the creek, after it was filtered of course. Then MD built a snowman, using lichen for a beard and an icicle for a nose. It was one of a kind. MD was so proud of his snowman.

Later that afternoon, we sat by the fire imagining eating spaghetti for dinner as we chewed down a PowerBar. We shared stories of the adventures we had during the day. We laughed and thanked God for watching over us as we had crossed those fallen trees over the water. It was a lot of fun.

The next morning, we packed up our gear and said our goodbyes to the beautiful surroundings that God had created just for us. We were so grateful for what we had there. I would love to come back to this place someday.

It was an amazing trip, one to remember, and MD loved it. Our last stop, as usual, was In-N-Out. After not eating much during our shortened winter trip, the hamburger, fries, and shake were so, so, so good.

MD, Andrew, & Dad

"15.12 Mile Bike Ride"

June 19, 2014

MD and I had been training for our Summer 60-mile bike trek in three weeks. Our training had been modified due to Andrew's desire to ride and train with us. I think that it is great! It is an opportunity for MD to be the big brother and set an example and for Andrew to get a taste of riding a bike on longer distances, especially at his age. MD is eight and Andrew is four years old.

Let's stop for a moment; if you have kids or remember as a kid at age four, bikes for a four-year-old have a 16-inch wheel, small cranks (with those little legs pedaling around and around just trying to catch up to everyone else), and are very heavy, beefy steel or aluminum frame, and only one gear with coaster brakes. Not ideal for long rides. These bikes are great for riding to school or around your neighborhood. But longer rides with hills… it is tough and most kids bail out. And remember those little legs pedaling for a long time. I am tired just visualizing it. There is even no place to put a water bottle on the frame so I have had to carry it on previous rides. However, thanks to Fred Gonzalez with Profile Design, I was able to put a rear water bottle mount on the side rails behind and under his saddle.

We decided to go for a short ride today… Well, we started at home and rode on Cathedral Oaks to Hollister Rd. to Ellwood School (three miles away) for a quick play on the playground. Then we hit Ellwood Bluffs on the trails and Andrew led the way since we had been riding out there several times together. From there we went to Deveroux along the scenic trail on the bluffs, then through Del Playa, then back on the trails around UCSB Lagoon. From there we connected to the bike path leading to Goleta Beach. We'd gone ten miles at this point. Andrew never complained and was eager to play at Goleta Beach and on the play structure. You'll notice in the photo where Andrew is on my chest that he looks tired. While we were there at Goleta Beach two ladies were playing their violins. It was a very nice and relaxing way to enjoy a few moments listening to wonderful music at the beach on a beautiful day. After powering down some PowerBars and ClifBars, we headed back on the bike path through UCSB and then to Stroke Rd over the freeway on Glenn Annie, turning up the small but painful hill on Cathedral Oaks to our house. Andrew never gave up and rode the whole way, except for some minor pushes during the last four miles when his legs were getting tired and he started to ride really slow. When we made it back to the house, we looked at the Garmin watch and it said 15.12 miles over about four hours of riding. Andrew claimed he was not tired, but he did fall asleep really quickly at 1900 hrs.

I was very impressed with both boys. MD, being the stronger of the boys, would ride ahead of us but then would wait for his little brother to catch up. He was a great leader. Both boys cheered each other on, even during the last four miles. Andrew would be yelling out, "MD, ride faster!" It was so much fun. Andrew wants to ride to Nana's house soon but I am not sure he knows what is in store for him. Andrew can be stubborn at times but it is what drives him to do great and amazing things like biking 15.12 miles.

I am a proud father. It will not be long when both boys stop and wait for me to catch up to them on Gibraltar road or some long ride. They are only going to get better, while I get a little bit older and slower.

Melody was happy to stay home while the boys and I went out riding.

Winter Backpacking Trip

"Embracing the Cold"

January 16-19, 2015

MD (eight years old) and I and our close and amazing friend Ben Parker set out again into the Western Sierra for four days. We picked up MD early from school on Friday and drove to Tamarack Lodge near Huntington Lake and stayed the night.

In the morning we set out for our grueling five and a half mile snowshoeing hike uphill that took us almost five hours to complete. We were exhausted. Ben found a spectacular base camp which was just perfect. The view was priceless. We set up our tent, made a big fire, and enjoyed the best tri-tip ever. We went to bed in our cozy, warm, minus 20-degree Mountain Hardwear sleeping bags.

We got up the next morning, had some sausage and eggs, did our morning Bible lesson, and then headed to West Lake by snowshoe. I kept saying to Ben and MD along the way that when I was here before the snow was fifteen feet deep unlike the one or two feet deep which we were in. Everything looked so different. There was an outhouse and a bear box that I had never seen before. When we reached West Lake, it was beautiful.

The lake had frozen over. MD and I were able to walk on the entire frozen lake. You could hear now and then the ice shifting. It was like when your stomach growls when you are hungry. It was eerie and exciting at the same time. We brought an ax and chipped away the ice about one and a half feet deep and reached water. Ben and MD filtered 9 liters of water and then MD tried fishing for a while. No catch. MD and I have watched many episodes of Man vs Wild where Bear Grylls (British Special Forces) would swim across freezing waters. Well, I wanted to try it, so I slowly went into the hole we dug in the ice. It was exhilarating. I could not feel a thing because the water was so cold which I think made it easier. I can see why hypothermia can set in so quickly.

After a minute or two in the frigid water, I got out and we headed back to base camp. Along the way, we crossed over meadows with running water underneath. So awesome. When we got back to base camp, we made our traditional snowman. We hung out, made another huge fire, ate some spaghetti, and went to bed.

The next morning, we woke up and had our Bible devotional time followed by awesome gluten-free pancakes by the fire, thanks to Ben. We packed up our gear and headed back to our car. Remember, it took almost five hours to get to base camp. We started off really slow—well, MD did. It took him 55 minutes to do one mile downhill. I think MD had a long trip and was just plain tired. Sometimes, he gets so focused or tunnel vision on one thing, like being tired, and nothing can motivate him, not even talking about Legos, Minecraft, or ice cream. This was not going to be fun going back. Ben and I made some negotiations with MD and a reward system for every mile for MD to help motivate him. Well, MD picked up the pace and we got back in exactly three hours to the car. Way to go MD! Thank the Lord because I do not think Ben and I could handle over five hours of hiking this slow.

It was an awesome trip, one to remember. This was MD's furthest trip backpacking in the winter. He is amazing. I love doing this with MD. It really bonds us together. I also really appreciated Ben for his patience and hard work. He is a team player with a servant's heart, and is the strongest Sherpa ever. He is a beast.

Because of the bond that I have with MD and the experience that he has gotten since he started backpacking at age four, I want to do the same for Andrew. Someday, Andrew will get to go. Andrew asks all the time when is it his turn. I am hoping this Summer that Andrew and I can go on a backpacking trip. Andrew is different than MD and needs a little bit more growing up before I take him on these wild and crazy winter trips.

We are going on another Winter trip in March with some new folks and MD really wants to go again. I look forward to March and hope there is even more snow to make our snow cave and live in it. More to come.

Winter Sierra Trip

"With Friend Roger Davids"

March 26-29, 2015

My friend Roger Davids and my sidekick son, MD, and I went to the Western Sierras for our Winter/Spring backpacking trip. It was a grueling hike with elevation starting around 7,230 feet to 8,849 feet through snow, ice, and dry trails. We drove up to Tamarack Lodge near Huntington Lake on Thursday night and spent the night. We left at 0700 and headed off on the trail. MD had not woken up yet, so the whining began and then continued for two miles. Oh, this was going to be a very long hike. But then MD got his game face on and was on a mission. At 5 1/2 miles, we stopped at our last camping spot in January with Ben, and MD and me. We took some staged pictures of MD "sleeping" where we had last set up our tent and sitting on a log to "warm" our hands where the fire pit had been.

We ate lunch there and then kept going. At about mile 6, MD asked Roger if he could carry some of Roger's gear on his pack to help Roger out. MD was motivated and strong. I was very impressed with Roger, for this was his first time backpacking in this kind of element. He never wavered but kept his pace up. We got to mile 6 1/2 and the trail got kind of confusing and not heading the way we needed, so we made our own trail. I told the boys from my previous experience in this area that the camp "was somewhere over there." Well, we got to the meadow but it was a mix of snow and water. We went around it but in hindsight, we should have gone around the other side. It took us a while to go around through the snow and thick woods and challenging terrain. We made it through and found West Lake.

Now, realize this. I had been here when snow covered the area. I did not know there were rocks the size of cars in front of the lake and continuing for about 250 meters past it. Now, if we were without 45-pound packs, no problem, maybe some effort. Oh, did I mention there was a meadow flowing with water in front of the big boulders, too? With our packs on, MD and I spent 30-40 minutes rock hopping, climbing over rocks trying to get to the other side. We finally made it. But where was Roger? He was still at the start of the big rocks. So, I went back to help him without my pack. We thought we could go around the other way which had fewer rocks but lots of snow. As we started around the entire lake, we stopped and thought, what if there was a small path around the boulders on the outside of the lake next to the flowing meadow. Duh! Sure enough, there was a path about one and a half feet wide, not all dry, but it took us only ten minutes maybe, if that.

We finally made it to the coolest and most beautiful campsite. It was right next to the lake with an incredible view. I looked at my Garmin watch—it said 8.76 miles, 6 hours and 28 minutes. Oh, my MOM! MD, Roger, and I made it! I had been wanting to make it to West Lake and camp for the past fourteen years but never made it, so this was a big deal for me. This was by far the furthest MD and I have done on any of our trips and he was amazing. His energy, encouragement, positive attitude, and perseverance was astonishing. He often on the hike would tell me the best part of this trip was being with me. Almost made me cry every time, I am tearing up as I write this.

After we set up camp, we found a fire pit nestled in between some rocks and trees. *This* was the place to hang out. We made a fire and started working on dinner. We also found a picnic table that was made from some of the fallen trees. Awesome. Comfort and a place to sit and eat. Well, by the time dinner was ready, tri-tip, rice, and veggies, we were so exhausted; I mean *really* exhausted. I could barely eat. The pictures of us eating at the picnic table were how we really felt. I could barely chew my food. I was done. MD ate most of his dinner, hiked back to the tent, and was asleep by 1700 and so was I around 1800. There left Roger, alone not knowing what to do since it was so early. I think he stayed by the fire and then went to bed at some point.

The next morning, we ate scrambled eggs with some left-over tri-tip and some veggies as well. Yummy to our tummies. We ventured off in the surrounding areas, tried fishing, hiked around the easy part of the lake, filtered 8 liters of water from the lake, and also made a log bridge across the meadow in front of the large car-size boulders.

Roger came up with this great idea. How about we try to find a shorter route back to the main trail. What a brilliant idea! Anything to shorten the trip back to the car would be fantastic. Well, out in the meadow in front of the large car-size boulders was this beautiful meadow about three football fields in length. Some areas were wet enough to walk in ankle-deep but others had a good amount of water running through them. In the meadow, we found orange clay pigeons and empty shotgun shells. I guessed this was the place to shoot guns during the summer. MD and I started collecting them and putting them in a plastic bag we found nearby. I think we collected twenty clay pigeons. We took them with us and put them on the trail we created in search of the main trail and to help us find our way back to camp. After about twenty minutes, we found the main trail which took off one and a half miles or so off our hike back home. AWESOME! It took us ten minutes to get back to camp. Loving this trail after what we had gone through on the way to our campsite.

We were so hot from the hike we decided to go into West Lake (35-40 degree temp). Well, let me clarify. Roger got his feet in and maybe up to his knees. MD found a log (200 meters away from us) which was the same log we had used on our last trip in January which we placed on the frozen lake to use as a bench to filter our water and fish in the ice hole we made. He had managed to push that log all the way back to us in the water, so he was up to his thighs deep in the water. I wanted to go in, but the water was so cold. So, I crossed over to one rock which caused me to go about waist deep.

By this point, I was thinking that I felt refreshed enough. But as I stood on the rock warming my body up by the sun's rays, I looked at another rock in the distance, about 25 meters. I had to do it! About ten minutes of convincing myself to do it, I did and it took my breath away. It was so cold, my whole body was numb. I climbed up on the rock and raised my arms with excitement and then the shivering and pain of the icy frigid water kicked in. I waved to Roger who was standing on the shore, nice and warm and cozy. My brain started to unfreeze and I realized I had to get back to shore. What was I thinking? Obviously I was not. I know what you are thinking. I have heard it before from you. "Shouldn't you think about this clearly before you go in?" I know, but I just had to do this. Well, I jumped back in and swam back to shore. I could hardly speak and shivered for about ten minutes. I was so thankful to be back on dry land. How does Bear Grylls do it on Man vs Wild? He makes it look so easy.

That evening we had spaghetti for dinner, hung out by the fire, and then went to bed. We got up in the morning, had some pancakes, packed up, and headed back to the car. We thought if it took almost 6 1/2 hours to get here it would take us 4 hours or so because it is downhill for the most part and we made a new trail that connected to the main trail. The boys tackled the trails with power, strength, and endurance. MD and I would say to each other when we were tired and our hips and feet hurt, "I can, I will, I'll do my very best through Christ who strengthens me!" (This is something I have taught my kids to say when things get hard and tough and can see no end.) We made it back to our car in one piece. I looked at my watch and it said 7.1 miles in 2 hours and 50 minutes. NO WAY! That was incredible. It took 3 hours in January with MD and Ben on our way back to the car and we had camped in 5 1/2 miles.

"This by far has been the best trip ever," according to MD. I was so proud of him and Roger for tackling this adventure. I am looking forward to going back this summer with MD, Andrew (yes Andrew, God help me), and my friend Mason Parker for a five-day backpacking trip. It was so beautiful there at West Lake and the journey to get there was priceless. I hope you enjoyed this lengthy story. I did not want you to miss out on the adventure of a lifetime.

Smiley Andy & Dad's Bike Trek

June 12, 2015

Andrew (five years old) and I went on a bike trek from Goleta, California, near Dos Pueblos High School to Carpinteria. We rode 30.6 miles in four hours and forty minutes which included stopping by Melody's work, lunch with Grandpa at his work, and several playground rest stops. Thanks to the professionals at Hazard's, like Matt who put on some fast tires for Andrew's bike, and Justin, a former employee at Hazard's who fixed Andrew's frame crank and brakes, and all the prayers from our family and church at Oaks Bible Church. We made it safely to Carpinteria.

We left around 0845 and "June gloom" was here which I was so thankful for because it would keep us cool on the road, and it was going to be a long ride on the saddle. We took Cathedral Oaks to

Glen Annie to Storke to the bike path through UCSB and Goleta Beach to Modoc, Las Positas, up the gnarly Cliff Drive hill, Shoreline to the Butterfly Beach into Montecito, then to Summerland, on Via Real to Padaro Lane back on Via Real and finally into Carpinteria, driving down Palm Rd to Carpinteria State Beach.

Andrew was amazing! He blew me away with his stamina, energy, drive, and persistence. He never wavered, but stayed steady and strong. When it got tough on the hills, he would say out loud, "I can, I will, I'll do my very best in Christ who strengthens me!" The last mile was tough but when we saw the State Beach he finished strong. I had never seen a five-year-old kid do such an incredible task like this. We had been training for months; his hardest ride was twenty-two miles when he was four, then a few weeks later turning five. He had so much fun and joy throughout the ride. I was so impressed and a very proud father.

We checked into the hike and bike (the last spot was taken). We set up camp and then headed off to the park/playground, lots of fun for Andrew, who still had tons of energy. Where does he get it from?

At our campsite, we met this really cool and humble Canadian named Philippe, nineteen years old from Montreal. He took a plane to San Francisco then got on his bike, alone, and headed South headed for Los Angeles in the next two days from now. I was so impressed and amazed. We invited him to dinner at The Palms which was really nice for all of us. After that we went to bed.

The next morning, we got up and ate at Esau's for breakfast. We came back to our tent, packed up, and headed back to the playground and then to the beach and played in the water. We had our favorite peanut butter and honey sandwich for lunch, yum! We showered off and headed to the train station. After waiting for a while, the train finally came, a little late. We landed in Goleta and were greeted by warm and loving smiles from MD and Melody. We made it back!

In the car heading home, MD and I were talking about our bike trek coming up. We were planning to ride from home to Ventura and back or take the train back, we weren't sure yet. Andrew jumped in the conversation and said, "I want to go!" Now all three of us have to decide what to do. Andrew is hooked. What had I gotten myself into? I will let you know in three weeks when we leave again for another wild adventure bike trek.

MD & Dad's 104-Mile Bike Trek from Goleta to Ventura & Back

June 24, 2015

After recovering from my 30.68-mile bike trek two weeks ago with Andrew (five years old), MD (nine years old), and I set off to attempt a 104-mile bike trek to Ventura and back. The first seventeen miles were a breeze; MD climbed Cliff Drive like it was nothing, leaving me in the dust. At mile seventeen we caught up with our friend Jenna from my work at Cottage Hospital, Tele floor. She rode with us all the way to Ventura and then she went on to Ojai and around Lake Casitas and back home. It was nice having her along for part of the ride to get to know her since she works the night shift. She grew up taking long bike trips with her dad so it meant a lot to her, which inspired her to do more with her dad.

On our way to Ventura, we stopped in Carpinteria for lunch and played at the play structure. We then traveled along the new bike path on Highway 101. So awesome! It was breathtaking seeing the ocean along the stretch of highway without worrying about a car hitting us. Between Sea Cliff and Mondos Beach, a fire broke out and the fire crew arrived about twenty minutes after it started. Scary! We have little water in California and everything is dry. We made it to Ventura's Emma Wood State Beach in five and a quarter hours, 46.01 miles. We were faced with strong winds and took us about forty-five minutes to set up our tent and get cozy.

After about two hours a group of campers arrived and kicked us out because it was their spot, and so we moved to a better place behind a large bush that kept the wind completely down. We walked down to the beach which took us only a few minutes. We enjoyed watching the waves come in but it was really windy. We headed back to our tent but then decided to explore the campsite area. We found an entrance into the bushes. As we walked along many pathways surrounded by ten-foot-tall dense bushes, we found what looked like homeless camps deep into the bush. Areas were cleared out to about thirty feet, with tents or other makeshift living situations. It was amazing what they had created to live in but at the same time, not very far from our campsite. I did not feel safe especially with my son and did not want anyone to steal our gear or bikes. While at our campsite, we noticed one man came through our campsite area carrying an empty Arrowhead water container and went to our bathrooms, walked out with a full container of water, and then took an outdoor shower along the outside of the bathroom for campers to use. He took his water and went back into the bushes to where he was living. I never left MD alone, especially to go to the bathroom or anywhere else for that matter. I was also frustrated that I had to pay $10.00/person to camp here where these homeless camps are using the facilities. It does not seem right or safe.

That night we had some spaghetti for dinner and prayed, thanking God for the wonderful time we were having as father and son. MD and I were very hungry after a long day of biking. We went to bed around 1830.

We got up around 0545 and had breakfast, packed up, and headed to our next camp at Carpinteria State Beach. I started having bike problems with awful grinding sounds coming from the crank, losing one gear at a time. Our route looked to be about eight miles short of our 100-mile goal, so we rode and climbed the hills of Carpinteria and looped back into town. Without my first three gears which makes it easier to climb up hills, it was tough, especially pulling a bike trailer. We set up camp, then played at the beach for hours with another father and his three boys who were car-camping there. Wonderful family. We then cleaned up and went to The Palms for dinner and came back and went to bed around 1900.

The next morning, we had breakfast at Esau's and stuffed our bellies. We packed up and rode in the hills of Carpinteria again to make up those lost miles. More gears grinding away, too. We landed on the Mesa to have lunch with Grandpa and then headed home, but had to stop to say hi to Melody at her work and bring her some lunch from the Mexican restaurant. As we approached Hollister and Storke/Glen Annie we had made it to 100 miles! I told MD that my crank was on its last stroke and any hill might do me in and I would be walking my bike and trailer home. He responded that we could get more miles in if we take Hollister and hopefully by the grace of God I will make it. So, we went up Hollister to Winchester and Sandpiper Golf Course and came around Cathedral Oaks. We arrived at our home with a total of 104 miles.

We did it! I was so impressed with MD. It was long and grueling at times. I asked him what his favorite part of the trip was. He said,

"Being with you, Dad, and the bike path along the 101 freeway, it was so smooth, no bumps!" As a father, it just makes you want to cry and thank God for this precious gift He has given me.

Stay tuned for the next adventure! In two weeks, both boys and I and our good friend, Mason Parker, will be backpacking for five days in the Sierras.

Western Sierra Backpacking Trip with the Boys & Mason Parker

On a Monday, MD and Andrew and our dear friend Mason Parker and I set off to the Western Sierras for five days of backpacking. We left in the morning and drove up to near Huntington Lake. We then took the Tamarack trail in my car until my SUV was unable to deal with the terrain. The boys and I got out of the car and Mason had this great idea and dropped his gear in the trees and drove back to the Tamarack Lodge. He then ran up and picked up his gear and then caught up with us. So nice to be young and in shape. He happens to be a cross-country runner, too.

As we hiked 2.5 miles up the trail, it gave me and the boys a chance to just talk and share in the suspense of what we would find and do at West Lake. They played with sticks along the way, taking their time which was just a perfect pace for all of us. I felt like MD was leading the way as his big brother for Smiley Andy as he held his hand, walking side by side. It was so precious to see them holding hands because as they grow older, this will become a distant memory. If you have kids or siblings, there is a love/hate relationship between brothers or sisters, unless I am the only one that has this in my family. My boys, I think they have a 40/60 love/hate brother relationship. Seeing them holding hands along the trail symbolized a love for each other in which I hope never separates. It was a beautiful thing to watch.

We finally reached West Lake, a total of 7.75 miles between the drive up the trail in my SUV and the hike in. We set up camp and embraced God's creation. It was beautiful. Mason finally arrived about an hour after us. I was so glad he found his way. The trails can be tricky, especially deciding which trail to take. We got out our collapsible fishing poles and fished, but caught nothing. We swam and played in the water to refresh our tired bodies. The boys spent most of the day in the water, keeping an eye on each other, another act of love for one another. They had fun playing together. They looked for big logs that were floating along the edge of the lake and then pushing them in the water and used them as canoes. That night we ate tri-tip, beans, and veggies. The boys went to bed in their tent and slept well while Mason and I had a chance to talk one on one about life, my kids, plans for the rest of the trip and just unwind from the long day.

The next morning, I went fishing and sure enough, I caught a rainbow trout. I had not caught a fish for a long time. I screamed and jumped up and down with excitement. While I was trying to catch more fish, off towards the distance, Mason was teaching the boys how to fish. I knew as a dad, there is a moment to teach your sons how to fish. But to see Mason teaching my two sons how to fish was so sweet and a precious moment for all of us. It gave Mason the opportunity to bond with my kids and for the kids to learn something new and cool for them even if it did not come from me. I enjoyed watching this process from a distance. Mason is so good with my two boys and these kids embraced it.

By noon we had two trout. We took the two trout and Mason taught all three of us how to clean a fish. It had been a long time since I did this, I think since junior high. We took our dehydrated vegetables and put them inside the fish, and used a leaf to tie the fish keeping the vegetables inside from spilling out. We then wrapped them in tin foil and cooked it inside our pot over the stove. We ate them for lunch and man oh man it was good and so fresh.

The kids played in the water and we took time to relax. In the afternoon we caught four more trout and ate them for dinner along with the BBQ chicken and rice and tortillas we were already having. Andrew wanted to be part of cleaning the fish. So, with Mason's help, he helped clean the fish and prepare it for cooking it in the pan. However, neither of the kids wanted to eat it. They told us, "We only eat what comes from the store." Even after explaining how the store gets the fish, they were not going to try it.

Wednesday morning came around and MD was not himself. He was so quiet! Not even talking about Legos or Minecraft. Something was wrong. So, I took him over to some rocks to hang out and talk and eat breakfast. He was still quiet and said his throat hurt and had a sore tummy. I was not sure what was up. He had backpacked with me on fourteen different trips and this was new and different. Usually on the hike up to basecamp is when he gets his headaches and tummy aches which last just that day. He sleeps for an hour or two then he is fine, but not days later. We headed back to camp and he stopped and threw up. We were about eight miles in the backcountry with horrible cell reception (Mason had his phone). We had a group discussion and decided that maybe we should pack up and head home.

Mason climbed up the side of a mountain to get a message to Melody that we were heading back. As the day went by MD perked up and was playing and laughing with his brother. Well, I guess he was better. So, I told Mason that we need to tell Melody we are staying. He showed me how to use his cell phone, and I took Andrew and we scrambled the same mountain Mason had to get a message to Melody. After an hour of trying, we headed back down and asked Mason to try "texting" (I had no clue how to do that since I do not have a cell phone). He got a message through later that afternoon. That night we enjoyed burritos, but then night got interesting and not because of the burritos. It started to rain and hail. We also had thunder and lightning. The thunder was about 3.5 seconds after the lightning. I was really nervous. The boys were fast asleep while I was worried, wondering if we should move somewhere else that might be safer.

Thursday morning finally came and it was still raining. Mason had his own tent while I shared the tent with the boys. After a couple of hours in the tent playing UNO and Legos, we were all getting antsy. I grabbed the boys and said we were going for a walk in the rain. Mason said he was going for a short five-mile run. Well, we hiked 3.5 miles round trip to Strawberry Lake. It was so beautiful! What an amazing lake. So different from West Lake. It is surrounded by huge granite rocks with the lake in the middle. There were dense trees unlike the open space you feel at West Lake. Tall grass alongside the lake unlike West Lake with more dirt.

We headed back to camp and the sky cleared up for about an hour. Then rain and hail unleashed upon us. We decided to pack up to take two days to get back to the car since it was about 7.75 miles. MD and Mason helped pack up Mason's tent and things while I was in our tent packing up leaving the tent standing. Oh, I forgot to tell you, Andrew fell asleep in a chair after we got back from the hike. Mason had to pick him up during the massive hail storm, still sleeping, and put him in the tent with me. It felt like hours went by, but finally, the storm settled. We finished packing and headed out. We got about four miles and the storm was back. We managed to find a small area in the midst of trees off the trail to set up the tent in the rain. It was a downpour.

We got the kids in the tent and then made a lean-to for the gear. We needed our gear off the ground and dry from the rain and it could not fit inside the tent. We took long branches and leaned them against a tree's branch that was about six feet from the ground. It was about five feet wide. We then piled branches with its leaves and placed them on the outside of the leaning branches with a footprint that came from the bottom of the tent as like a tarp to make it watertight, so as the rain came down it would run off the leaning structure and keep whatever was underneath it dry. Then we stacked horizontal branches inside the lean-to making a platform to put the gear on and keep it dry and out of the rain. It worked. Mason made dinner while I set up the sleeping bags and pads in the tent. Now, remember, we have two tents. We decided to just set up one tent because there was not enough room to set up two tents in this thick forest that we were in and have all four of us in a three-man tent. I think Andrew was the only one who slept. It was so tight and Mason and I had to lay on one side for the whole night.

Friday was a new day. The temperature in the mid-30's, we ate some oatmeal and packed up and headed for the car. We were all tired but made it to the car with no rain.

I was so proud of the boys, especially Andrew since this was his first backpacking trip. He was awesome. Never really complained about all the hiking. Stayed steady and strong. He helped set up and take down the tent, prepared meals, did dishes, and embraced every moment. I was so proud of him. He really surprised me and Mason. We thought it was going to turn out differently, like when he got tired if he would stop and not move a muscle, but he did not. The first three days were tough for MD, who had not been feeling so well. But after those three days, all he talked about was Minecraft. Mason was perfect for him because he knows what he is talking about, unlike his dad.

It was a great trip with my boys and Mason. We experienced so many challenges. We prayed a lot and God was faithful and answered all our prayers. I feel my faith in the Lord grew to enable me to trust Him more in the midst of the storm.

Western Sierra Trip with Me, MD, Mason Parker, & Keefe Hansen

"Good Friends Sharing a Backpacking Trip"

February 11-15, 2016

On Thursday, my son MD (nine years old) and our friends Mason Parker and Keefe Hansen and I headed off to the Western Sierras. MD and I drove up after he got out of school. Mason and Keefe drove up later and met us at the Tamarack Lodge. We slept there for one night to acclimate to the high altitude.

In the morning we had breakfast and then MD did the dishes while we packed up our gear. We headed off around 0830 and took the trails and headed for West Lake (7.75 miles). Keefe and Mason went by snowshoes and MD and I went by cross-country skis made by Rossignol and Madshus. For Christmas, my lovely wife and my wonderful in-laws bought me a Pulk sled (thanks Grant and Ashley from PulkSled.com). It was great! It spared me from putting a pack on since my recent neck surgery "went so well" (not!). It was a challenge by skis to haul it uphill with icy snow trail conditions, but doable.

After a half-mile on skis, MD and I decided to switch to our MSR snowshoes because we were sliding all over the place and slowing the group down. MD had had to learn how to ski right out of the gate, so to speak. He had nowhere to practice beforehand. As a child learning a new skill, it was frustrating and he had a couple of moments of getting mad and not wanting to go any further, but slowly and surely he did it until we switched gear. The snowshoes gripped the ice and I was able to pull the sled. At mile two, MD wanted to test out the sled, but he only moved it five inches. Keefe wanted to give the sled a try too, I did not refuse. Later Mason pulled it as well. Everybody pitched in, thanks, guys.

During our trek, MD struggled to keep going because he had a really bad headache and tummy ache. So, we stopped at five miles to

set up camp where we had before. I looked at my watch, which said six hours of being on the trail—it usually takes three). I could not believe it. I was wondering why I was so tired. We'd come to learn that MD usually struggles at high altitudes with headaches and stomachaches. I've tried to prepare him beforehand to prevent these but a child at this age just can't see that far in advance. And then it's hard to get him to drink enough while hiking. As a dad,

I have had a couple of tough talks with him to discuss the challenges of what happens when he gets into this state, and how it affects the trip and people involved. He's trying to learn, and I'm learning that I need to be more patient with him when I see his symptoms emerging.

Despite the long hours, it was worth it. The view was amazing and there was tons of snow. We got a Nemo pad out and MD laid on that and fell asleep for an hour and a half, never moving a muscle. The rest of us set up base camp, setting up the Marmot Thor 3 tent, building a snow cave, a fire pit, and getting firewood and the kitchen area prepared. Lots to do the first day. For dinner, we had the best tri-tip we had ever had. The guys slept in the tent (as the snow cave was not ready yet) and I slept in my Outdoor Research bivy which is like a waterproof outer shell that the sleeping bag and sleeping pad goes inside and keeps you dry and protected from the elements. It is super lightweight and compact. Great to have in an emergency. It worked well so we did not have to bring another tent. If you are claustrophobic, a tent is much better. More spacious and you can move around inside a tent.

Morning came by quickly. I got the fire going and breakfast was started thanks to Mason; yummy eggs and some left-over tri-tip. After breakfast, we worked on our base camp. We all needed a break, so MD and I headed off on our skis while Keefe and Mason explored on their own. MD impressed me so much on the skis, especially because he had never really done it before. He was fearless hitting the hills with grace and speed.

Cross-country skiing is more versatile than alpine skiing. These skis have fish scales on the bottom, underfoot mainly that allow you to move forward and keep you from sliding backward. Your boots are secured to the ski at the tip of the boots, allowing you to move your heel up and down to help you glide the skis across the snow. Downhill can be tricky because your boot is not fully secured to the binding, allowing for movement side to side and up and down on the skis which can make you unbalanced. At times, there is lots of falling because of losing your balance. After a couple of hours, we came back and worked around camp.

We started something new for MD and me. We did some journal writing while others went off on their own to have some time for themselves. MD and I got my Bible and did a devotional by reading some scripture and then together wrote in a journal. Journal writing has never been appealing to me. I never liked journal writing as a kid, especially in school, forced to write something profound in a journal for fifteen minutes. I have dyslexia and a reading disability so having to write my thoughts down takes lots and lots of effort and concentration and I am so critical about my writing and do not like misspelling words, jumbling my words, or messy handwriting. I am just not a fan of it. But during this trip, I forced myself to journal as a way to document my adventures or write down my thoughts which I might not communicate out loud to others. It was not an easy task, just like writing this book. Writing this book is a big deal for me. I am blown away that I have accomplished so much with writing this book for others to enjoy. A huge landmark and benchmark in my life. I think writing in a journal opened a new door for me and to incorporate my son with it. MD has very similar learning disabilities like mine so pushing ourselves is an achievement. It is also a way to encourage each other. We can write whatever we want; a lot or just a sentence. It did not matter. What mattered was just trying it. It was cool.

Mason and Keefe had their chance for quiet time as well. Keefe found a large boulder and spent time reading his Bible and praying. Mason, I think, had a nap in the tent. We agree these trips are important to us, to be able to take the time and be still, reflect, and embrace the beauty that God has created around us. We listen to the voice of God through reading His Word, engaging prayer, and meditation. We have great conversations about life and how our walk with the Lord is going. We have a sense of accountability to each other, and I am very grateful for that.

At dinner, we ate BBQ chicken with rice, beans, tortillas, and veggies all while hanging out by the fire. We all headed to bed. I went back to my bivy to sleep and the others slept in their Mountain Hardwear sleeping bags in the new snow cave. Unlike last time, MD slept through the night in the much bigger snow cave.

Sunday morning was so peaceful and quiet. The guys were still sleeping in the snow cave while I started the fire and made our breakfast of delicious pancakes. Keefe had to leave because he needed to be home with his family as his wife is going back to work on Tuesday after being on maternity leave. Such a good husband. We said our goodbyes and he headed back to his car, five miles away.

MD was on a mission today. He cut down branches and hauled them in the pulk sled to the fire area. He wanted to make sure we had enough firewood for tonight's fire. He did this all on his own with no prompting from any of us, really.

When MD's mission was completed, we decided to snowshoe to West Lake by taking a different route told to us by Mayor Mark, a local guy who was snowmobiling and stopped by our camp the day before. It was a very steep, long two hills. MD was done, but there was light at the tunnel and could see West Lake in the distance.

We made it to West Lake and it was covered with snow. It was priceless. The picnic table where we had eaten before at West Lake was buried in the snow; no evidence it was there. We played around on the frozen lake but then had to head back because it was getting late. It was a breeze going back, all downhill. MD liked that a lot. Mason went ahead of us to get dinner ready and a fire started because it was getting late. I was so glad to be back after snowshoeing five miles. I was so tired and looking forward to eating dinner, sitting by the fire, and enjoying my last night here before we would leave in the morning.

When I arrived, Mason asked me, "Do you want the good news or the bad news? Good news, you guys made it back fast, only twenty minutes behind me. Bad news, my sleeping bag is soaked from the roof of the snow cave inside." I never imagined this would happen because it was cold and windy today. We pulled the rest of the gear out and Mason put a 1L water bottle inside the cave where it was dripping. Within thirty minutes the bottle was full. We were gone for four hours, so there was a lot of water in his sleeping bag. Mason was so kind to make dinner and I packed up the gear. We left at 1800 and headed back to the car, another five miles away. The sun was setting with the most beautiful skies of the trip and then it was dark. MD and I skied back to the car while Mason snowshoed, pulling the last three miles with the pulk sled so I could keep up with MD on the skis and spend some one-on-one time. Some of the hills we skied on were steep and fast. I could not get over how well MD did. I had a hard time catching him, he was so fast and absolutely no fear in him. A drastic transformation from our way up to camp! We made it back to the car around 1915. We packed up, called my wife, and told her we are heading back. We ate dinner at our traditional In-N-Out and arrived home at 0115. MD went to bed around 0215 and I finally crawled into bed at 0330.

It was an awesome trip. Everyone was safe, and we had a great time. It was great bonding with my son and the two guys. It was a blessing to have Keefe come on his first trip with us. He is a hard worker and laid back when he needs to be. He is thoughtful and above all, puts his marriage first. What a great example to head back home to his wife during a fantastic trip with a bunch of guys.

Mason is like part of my family. He and MD have a special connection. Mason makes a huge effort to talk with MD and engage in all sorts of discussions from sports, Legos, the video game Minecraft, and school. This helps a lot when MD gets tired of hiking and keeps him moving. I really appreciate Mason, not only for his friendship but the bond he has established with MD.

Thank you to my wife Melody for helping me buy and prep the food (like the cookies and brownies for Daryl, the manager of the Tamarack Lodge, so we can park there for four days). Thank you for letting me go on these trips with my kids and entrusting me with them. Thank you, friends and family, for your prayers and support. Thank you to Gear Companies for your awesome gear to keep us fueled, safe, more efficient, warm, and protected.

I am exhausted, so this concludes my story. I hope you did not fall asleep reading this.

2-13-

ToDay we went Skiing and went down hills (it was fun).
—MD

2-14-16

toDay was a bad Day. First, I go to west lake it was a hard hike in the snow. When we got back every thing was wet so we had to leave,
—MD

Andrew's 1st Winter Sierra Trip with Dad

February 26-29, 2016

This was by far one of the most epic winter backpacking trips I have ever experienced and it was with my son, Andrew, and it so happens that it was his first winter backpacking trip. Two weeks ago, I met this guy named Mayor Mark of Tamarack who had driven up to our base camp by snowmobile and told me to call him the next time I came up on our winter backpacking trip. The funny thing about Mayor Mark is that I met him long ago on one of my first backpacking trips. I was driving around a side street near the Huntington Lake area by the Tamarack Lodge. Mayor Mark was driving a tractor pushing snow off the roads. I stopped him and asked where to park. Unknown to us, we would meet again and become friends, and he would be a part of my backpacking memories with my children.

I connected with Mayor Mark prior to coming up and asked for some help. I took Andrew out of school on Friday and drove to near Huntington Lake in the Western Sierras. We parked at Tamarack Lodge as usual, with brownies and chocolate chips for Daryl, the Manager at the lodge, who lets us park there. When we arrived, Major Mark was there with his snowmobile ready to take us to our base camp five miles away. I got to drive it!

Most of the time Mayor Mark drove while Andrew and I hung on for our lives. Mark was on one side and me on the other with Andrew behind. It was a bit awkward and at one point I lost my balance, fell off, and the snowmobile almost rolled onto me. It was a learning curve! It's all about balance and weight distribution as we went over or around rolling trails and bumps of snow. If the balance is off, the snowmobile can go off course, so getting three people to work together on something when two were new was a challenge. But wow, I love the feeling of the fresh cold mountain snow air in my face at 30 mph! And it really cut our travel time.

We arrived at the base camp we used two weeks ago and boy, did I feel energized that I had not spent all my energy snowshoeing while pulling a pulk sled to this place. It was fantastic. We said our goodbyes to Mayor Mark while Andrew and I got to work building our tent, setting up our kitchen and fire pit, and our new snow cave per Andrew's request—more like insisted upon. I found Andrew crashed out in the snow cave several hours into setting up base camp. I think he was tired from all the work he had done. He woke up when it was dinner time. Had the famous tri-tip, beans, rice, veggies, and tortillas. We did the dishes and then went to bed in our new snow cave.

The next morning at dawn, I was awakened by a kid saying, "Time to get up and make eggs and then go sledding and skiing." So, I got up and we did just that. We had a blast sledding down this huge hill. The pictures do not do it justice. The GoPro videos are hilarious and I still laugh with tears running down my face watching it. After that, we cross-country skied about 0.85 miles. Andrew did awesome for his first time. I was so proud of him. After all our adventures we took an afternoon nap. We then had dinner, spaghetti of course, and to my surprise, Andrew started doing the dishes on his own. He would not even let me help out. I kept asking myself, who is this kid? I think he really captured the essence of camp life. He was so in tune with me and listened to my every word as I tried to teach him the basics of winter backpacking. He really took it to heart and applied it. He was in tune with the environment and that he was learning important lessons from me about winter camping. I could tell he just "got it" and realized some of the lessons were for safety. He was very attentive and demonstrated his new skills well. He is a great kid to go camping with and I was very comfortable with him.

We chose to sleep in the tent that night, and the next morning we packed our gear and headed down the mountain with our snowshoes on until we could ski. It was another beautiful day and we made our five-mile trek back. After about four miles, Andrew was tired so I let him sit in the saucer sled behind the pulk sled as I pulled it while on my skis. He enjoyed that. We made it back to our car in about 2.5 hours. We loaded the gear in the car and headed for home, but had to make a pit stop at In-N-Out.

It was a wonderful bonding time with Andrew. I am so thankful it went so well. It could have been a very stressful time. Winter camping is a whole different element in which you have to respect nature and be prepared. A five-year-old in this element could have some challenges. There were hard parts that Andrew had to work through, tiring easily, complaining something is too hard, the repeated asking, "how much longer..." Both of my boys at this age need extra help with basic things like tying snow boots, putting on gloves, and even getting dressed because of all the layers. But both are excited to be outside and experience the new sights and feelings and want to explore and play and have fun. MD never had the experience at this young age to do the snowmobile, so Andrew had that advantage, and MD had to work harder. But they have both loved the experience and I'm so very grateful. And I never have to tell them to get into bed when we're camping!

Some of my favorite moments with Andrew were when we would have our daily devotions in the Scriptures and talk about it. I also wrote in my journal and he wanted to be a part of it too, and wrote down his thoughts. In reflection, safety with the kids is the most important thing. I have to constantly be on top of their hydration, heat, and activities. It's similar when we go to the beach—they need sunscreen, I have to be aware of waves and current of the ocean, and prevent sand from getting in their eyes, for example. The basic needs of a child are simple, and with the right equipment and experience, a winter trip can be fun, safe, and a great adventure.

I look forward to next year and maybe both of my boys can go with me at the same time. I really cherish my relationship with my kids. I am so thankful they like the outdoors like me.

The Boys Summer Western Sierra Trip

June 27, 2016

Summer had come and it was time for another backpacking trip to the Sierras with my two boys, now aged six and ten. I had Sunday to spend with Melody and then the boys and I headed for Huntington Lake at 0508 on Monday morning and arrived at 1008. When we arrived, our local friend up there, Mayor Mark, graciously had an off-road vehicle, with roll bars and helmets to take us up to our base camp at West Lake 7.75 miles away. It was a blessing since it was already 80 degrees and it probably would have taken us all day to get there with the high elevation.

We all had fun driving up there and Andrew managed to fall asleep on the way there. Let me tell you, the terrain was harsh. When we got there, we said our goodbyes to Mayor Mark and invited him to come back for dinner. I set up our base camp while the kids played in the water. I joined them after I was done and the kids were riding logs like canoes in the lake. So cool and creative. The kids decided to go and play Uno in the tent and I went fishing, so relaxing. We each had a radio to keep in touch but Andrew definitely used it too often to tattle on his big brother. Melody and I teach them to be respectful but they argued a lot today. By 1700, I came back to camp and made dinner, tri-tip, beans, rice, veggies, and tortillas. By 1800, Mayor Mark and his son, Dominic, joined us for dinner. It was great to fellowship with them. After dinner, Mayor Mark and his son left and we went to bed.

The next morning, I made some eggs, veggies, and left-over tri-tip. The boys wanted to eat in the tent because they were in the middle of a game of Uno. I ate outside. After breakfast, we were back in the water and fishing, where I caught five nice-sized rainbow trout. I cooked some of the fish for us for lunch but the kids once again refused and said they only eat fish bought from the store. These kids do not know how good fresh fish is. During the afternoon, a storm came through, thunder and lightning. It did not last very long. It was nice to have the rain. I built a lean-to tarp for our gear and MD made a huge fire. Evening came and we made burritos for dinner, which MD thought were the best ever, plus leftover brownies and cookies. Then we went to bed.

I used my awesome flint and with dry wood and in ten minutes I had a fire going. The smell of pancakes woke the boys in the morning to come out to eat. Afterward, we played a game of checkers, then went and hung out at the lake. MD caught a trout and so did I. We kept them alive and made a fish pond and the kids enjoyed watching them closely. By noon, we decided to hike to Strawberry Lake, around a four-mile round trip. It was hot and uphill so we took a lot of breaks. When we got there, it was so beautiful with the tall grass, the flowers, and the dragonflies everywhere. There was a rock in the lake with a tree growing at the top of it and flowers. The boys figured out a way to climb a log and get on top of the rock. MD found the stream that fed the lake, and the very cold water helped soothe his mosquito bites. Andrew, while wading in the lake, got his Croc shoe stuck in the thick mud and none of us could get it out. Thankfully I'd packed another set of shoes. They had lots of fun. We headed back a couple of hours later to base camp at West Lake.

It was almost unbearably hot. MD came up to me and said we should leave today to split up the hike for Andrew since it might be difficult for him. I thought that was so sweet. So, we decided to do that. I packed up and made spaghetti for dinner. Around 1730, we hiked out. We followed the trail until we decided to take a shortcut that we used on our last winter trip. Well, we could not find it until we saw the remnants of a sign on the ground with the letter M and J and an arrow, made by our friend Mason on our last winter trip with Mason and MD in February. I could not believe it was still there. When we looked at the direction where to go, there was no trail.

We decided to try it. We bushwhacked two miles up the difficult uphill terrain, where we finally caught up with an existing trail. We had about four miles left for the hike and it was 1930. I told the boys we should make a camping site nearby and rest until the next morning. We voted and I lost. The boys wanted to keep on going and head back to the car. They were on a mission. Andrew started to struggle with his pack, so I took MD's and MD took Andrew's, and we kept going. Andrew would run ahead of us and then jump out and scare us when we got close. It really kept him motivated, and us too, because we were all so tired. We were about a mile away from our car and again I suggested we camp near the creek and freshen up, go to bed and start in the morning. We voted and I lost.

We made it back to the car at 2100. The boys and I did ten miles of hiking in one day. I could not believe it! I called Melody from the Tamarack Lodge where we kept our car and told her that we were heading back. So, we did but had to make our traditional stop at In-N-Out. We were the only ones in the restaurant. Andrew got an employee badge and a hat from a worker whose name was also Andrew. The food was quick! That drive home was brutal; I had to stop a couple of times to do jumping jacks on the side of the road to stay awake. We finally arrived home at 0300 and went to bed.

I was so impressed with my kids and the teamwork they showed on the hike back. They were encouraging, supportive, motivated, and never quit. Although at base camp, they gave each other a hard time and picked on each other, they had lots of fun playing games, climbing on rocks, and paddling with their logs that they found. They also really worked well together as a team when the trail got rough. We learned that card and board games can really help build relationships, even if you lose.

God had kept us safe, provided great weather, protection from the elements, and kept the bears and mountain lions far away. The only issue we had was the nasty mosquitos. Andrew won the prize for the most bites, ranging somewhere around seventy or so. His face and neck took the brunt of it. They were relentless! Neither the fire nor a Bounce sheet helped keep them away, the spray was a little better. Finding that old sign (letters M and J and arrow) for the trail shortcut was such a blessing, and I thank God for keeping us on the right path.

I am blessed to have these boys in my life. It was great to bond with them and get them in nature. I really enjoyed the relaxing and therapeutic time fishing alone. In two weeks, we leave for a 60-mile bike trek down South. It should be lots of fun.

Summer Bike Trek with a Wonderful Ending

July 11-12, 2016

After MD, Smiley Andy, and I recovered from our recent back-packing trip in the Sierras, we left Monday for our annual bike trek for three days covering 60 miles. However, I had an appointment with a surgeon this past Monday to have a trigger finger release of my right middle finger. I have been dealing with this finger for a long time and it would get stuck in a curled position and was very painful to straighten out. I have had several injections of cortisone to reduce the swelling and inflammation but now was the time to have it fixed. As a nurse, I use my hands all the time from helping patients get out of bed, handling medications and equipment, and charting on the computer. It also affected me in my everyday life. From sports activities like rock climbing to stand up paddleboarding, biking, and simple things like grabbing a cup in the kitchen or opening a cabinet. When I would wake up in the morning, my finger would be stuck in a closed position and it was so painful to release it and straighten it out. So, the surgeon told me that this Wednesday I will have surgery at GVCH. I told him I will be on a three-day bike trek with my two boys. I left the appointment and spoke to my family and we made a unanimous decision to go for only two days and have Melody pick us up at our destination and then take us home.

We got on our bikes and headed 30 miles from the end of Goleta to Carpinteria at 1030. It was already in the 70s on a clear and beautiful day. We were feeling good and strong. At mile five, we were stopped by a KEYT3 news reporter named Vicky Nguyen. She interviewed us about the new Goleta Beach Bridge and that night it was aired. If you search online for "KEYT Goleta Beach Bridge," you can see it. Finally, cyclists and pedestrians can feel more safe traveling from the bike path to cross the street and back on the path to go over the bridge. It has always been a dangerous spot. I look forward to seeing it completed and I appreciate the City of Goleta seeing the need to fix this serious problem.

After several hours on our bikes, we came to the notorious hill, Cliff Drive. MD flew up the hill on his road bike and waited about ten minutes before Andrew and I arrived. We made a pit stop at my father-in-law, Greg's work for lunch. After we were refueled, we headed on. When we reached Summerland, we saw my uncle Randy walking his dog on the road so we said hi. Then we were passed by three guys who were riding from Victoria, Canada, and heading to San Diego. They were also stopping at Carpinteria for the night. We had a chance to hang out with them at the beach in Carpinteria and hear from them about their journey so far, amazing!

We reached Carpinteria State Beach after five hours including our lunch break of forty-five minutes. The "hike and bike" area is shared with all sorts of people, including the homeless. There were some folks who were intoxicated, smoking cigarettes, and doing drugs. I went to the kiosk and explained the situation and they were kind and thoughtful and moved us to a safer and more appropriate place to camp. The boys and I worked together to set up camp and then headed to the beach. We were getting hungry, so we came back to camp and MD learned how to set up the stove. Both boys cooked our dinner and then afterward we went out for ice cream; they deserved it. Afterward, we walked back to camp and crawled into bed.

The next morning, the kids slept in (0730) and I hung around camp and talked with the guys who were biking from Canada. Next to us were also a father and son who biked from Alaska. You meet the most wonderful and inspiring people on bikes. Someday, I would love to do that with my boys. The boys got dressed and we ate at Esau's Restaurant and filled our bellies. Next, we went and played at the beach for several hours, then came back and packed up. I had thought that we had to be out of our campsite at 1400, but when we came back to our campsite there was a notice form from the Ranger Station that said I will be cited for staying past 1200. Oops! I went to the kiosk and apologized profusely and they showed grace to me and let me leave without any fines. We ate lunch and then went to the kid's favorite playground where we played tag for hours. We also sat on the grass and played UNO. Of course, Andrew won three times. He is so good at this game.

Melody arrived at 1845 after having to sit in an hour of stop and go traffic. I loaded the SUV with our gear and loaded the bikes on the Thule bike rack. We went to dinner at The Palms where you cook your own meat. The boys love to do that. This is the first trip with my boys that Melody joined us. It was great to have the whole family together. It was also a wonderful way to end the trip.

I woke up at 0450 this morning and walked to my in-laws' house 3.2 miles away and my father-in-law, in the kindness of his heart, drove me to GVCH at 0535 to have surgery on my right finger. I am recovering, just dealing with pain, swelling, and some stiffness. Thank goodness for pain meds and ice.

I absolutely love being a dad and so truly blessed to share these adventures with my children. It is a privilege. I also appreciate my dear and precious bride for entrusting me and allowing me to take our kids on these adventures.

Did Someone Say Bike?
Santa Barbara 100

October 22, 2016

Today was a big deal for MD (ten years old) as he entered his first bike ride event, the Ride Santa Barbara 100. According to the Ride Santa Barbara 100 website, "The Ride Santa Barbara 100 takes place in one of the most beautiful and challenging locations in the United States. We offer four distinct courses to suit every cyclist's ability – each course offering a world-class Santa Barbara cycling experience." MD joined a local team called RYBT (Riviera Youth Bike Team). A friend of mine named Zach Bertges saw a need in the city to help kids who were troubled or at-risk kids. Zack reached out to our local organizations such as the Center for Alcohol Drug Abuse (CADA), Child Abuse Listening Mediation (CALM), the Franklin Youth Center, and local Boys and Girls clubs. Zack would take these at-risk kids from ten- to thirteen-years-old (some of which had never ridden a bike, in the beginning) and teach and train them how to ride a bike and then train them to ride the Race SB100.

Zack knew that MD loved to bike and thought his influence and mine could make an impact in these kids' lives, so we joined them. These kids, including MD, have been training very hard—three days a week for several months including a one-hour spinning class on Tuesdays, one hour of drills on Thursdays, and riding for two hours on Saturdays.

The SB100 has different distances and the RYBT rode the 34-mile race. "The 34-mile course gives the riders a taste of what Santa Barbara cycling has to offer. Starting along the idyllic, palm-lined beaches of the Santa Barbara Waterfront, you'll ride through some of the most exclusive neighborhoods in the country before turning inland to experience the back roads and rolling foothills of Santa Barbara with a few short climbs along the way. The course finishes with a gorgeous tour of exclusive Hope Ranch, then back to the finish line at Leadbetter Beach. There are two aid stations on the 34-mile route. With a total altitude gain of 2,200 feet, this course is suitable for a beginner to intermediate cyclist", according to their website.

We started at 0800 in the foggy Santa Barbara marine layer at Leadbetter Beach, riding to Montecito, climbing San Ysidro to Mountain Dr, down Ashley to Sycamore Canyon, climbed Cold Spring Rd (passing a familiar estate at 1030 Cold Spring Rd) to Mountain Dr, then made our way down to 192 at Sheffield Reservoir to Foothill Rd/Cathedral Oaks, turning left at Foothill School/ Community Covenant Church, connecting to the bike path leading under the freeway, left on the bike path to Modoc Rd and then through Hope Ranch. There we were met by our fans in vehicles: my sister Stephanie with her son Paysen and my son Andrew, then followed by Melody in her car. They cheered us on as we were coming to the finish line just five miles away.

After riding through Hope Ranch, we landed down at Hendry's Beach and faced the grueling last climb up Cliff Dr. MD and I have had a tradition to see who can get to the top first, and I was not going to be second. We had asked the RYBT head coach if we could pass our team and race to the top and he said ok. MD flew up the hill passing other riders in the race, and unfortunately, MD beat me by a wheel length to the top at the stoplight. He was very proud to hold his "title" of again beating his dad up the hill. From there we rode down Shoreline Dr. to the finish line at Leadbetter Beach with lots of spectators cheering us on for completing our race in 4 hours 36 minutes (which included two 30-minute rest stops and breaks to have everyone riding together). We all finished the race together, which demonstrated that we had trained well together as a team, we finished this huge accomplishment as a team.

It was a great and proud day for both of us. MD and I enjoyed every moment. I appreciated the support from our family and the riders that came along during the race cheering on my son and the other young riders on our team. Yesterday, the temperature was 98 degrees, but today it was in the 70's and low 80's. So thankful for that.

By the way, until last week, MD had been riding a 24" road bike and the head coach said he had outgrown it. No way! Bikes are expensive and he has only had this for two summers and he has a race in one week. I could not find anything on Craigslist or at any bike shops, so I put him on my 48cm bike… Well, it fits him and now I am out of a bike. Sad for me but a proud moment too that my son is growing up. I sure love being a dad.

Winter Backpacking Trip

January 13-16, 2017

WOW! AMAZING! BREATHTAKING!

I had decided to branch out of my typical winter backpacking trips by taking just a couple of people to try to guide groups. It was a passion for me. I want to share with others the beauty that comes from winter backpacking and what it brings to the individual. I get so much joy from it. I have this trip, one in February, and possibly another in March.

This was one of the most beautiful winter trips that I have ever experienced in the past sixteen years of winter backpacking. For the past two weeks, I have been looking at the weather reports and it has been dumping tons of snow and an open window of clear skies showed for the dates of my trip. Thank you, God.

I left with a group of five outdoor enthusiasts. One was David Brown, a great nurse and friend who drove down from Washington.

We have known each other since our Santa Barbara High School days. We graduated together in 1990. Later we worked together on a tele/cardiac floor at Cottage Hospital before he transferred to ICU, became a dialysis nurse, and then moved to Washington. We have kept in touch since then which has been great. He loves the outdoors and loves to hike. He has backpacking experience but had never gone winter camping.

Tessa Lippmann and her son, Jan (eleven years old) live down the street from my mom's house. Her husband, Kevin, and I went to high school together and both of us had a love for tennis which we both played. I am not sure how I met Tessa, maybe through Kevin. We started talking about backpacking and skiing. They absolutely love the outdoors. They kite surf, ski, play tennis… you name it, they do it; except for winter backpacking.

They never sit still, always on the go on their next adventure. Everyone in their family is incredible, professional-level skiers. I could never in my lifetime be as good as they are. Even their kids ride double black diamond runs. I am still on greens and sometimes blues. As we talked more, she seemed very interested and excited to go on a winter backpacking trip. Her family had never done this before. This was their first time winter backpacking.

MD is ten years old and this is his eighth winter backpacking trip. Now he is comfortable in his surroundings and loves the outdoors which makes it fun to do together as father and son.

On Friday early in the morning, we headed toward the Western Sierras near Huntington Lake. We all piled into one van, thanks to Tessa, and spent seven hours getting to know each other on the drive up. It was a longer than normal drive because of a couple of stops and conditions. Tessa got pulled by a CHP officer in Santa Maria and didn't have her registration, but the officer only gave her a fix-it ticket for that and not for the speeding she had been doing. Oops. We stopped at In-N-Out for lunch and tried to help a family jump start their car, but we were unsuccessful. As we got close to Tamarack

Lodge we needed to stop to put chains on. The right chain broke so we only had the left, which also broke two straps, but we finally arrived at the Lodge, ate dinner, and headed off to bed.

We woke up around 0545 and were on the trail by 0728 with temperatures in the teens. There was snow everywhere, fresh deep powder on the ground, and in the trees cradled by the branches. It was magical.

Tessa with skis and I with snowshoes pulled pulk sleds thanks to Grant and Amy from Minnesota (skipulk.com) who designed these amazing sleds to carry our gear. On snowshoes, David carried his pack. MD had his snowshoes on while Jan was on his fast alpine touring skis. The snow was so deep it made it a challenge to pull the pulk sleds through the snow. Our destination was West Lake, about 8.5 miles on the longer route due to the steep terrain and deep snow. We stopped at 5.75 miles, which took 7.5 hours, at one of my favorite base camps at West Lake. It has a beautiful view and there were rocks surrounding our shelter. This was the toughest snowshoe or ski hike ever for me. It was grueling, challenging, painful at times. I was looking to others for a source of strength, and praying to God frequently to just get me to the next rest stop. The whole team was exhausted, except for Tessa who could have gone another 5+ miles. I do not think she even had a bead of sweat on her forehead. She was so strong and powerful.

We set up base camp as usual with the tents, the kitchen area, and a temporary living room with a campfire setting. It was great having three adults really working hard after a long day to set up camp. The boys were very tired. I find it more comfortable and ideal to have a kitchen area that is chest high so you can cook easily. I dig out the snow and make a countertop level area to put the stove, fuel, cooking utensils and dishes, and food (which is off the ground) on it. It also saves my back so I'm not bending over and or sitting on the ground but standing up. I also place pine branches where I stand to keep my boots off the snow which helps keep my feet a little bit warmer. When we gathered around the fire pit, it was nice to have a seating area that I made out of snow and cut out a couch-like seating arrangement and placed pine branches to sit on and below for our feet to keep them dry and off the snow. It is homier that way, too.

While we were doing all this, MD, exhausted and suffering from a headache and stomach ache, fell asleep on a tarp for about an hour and then he was refreshed to keep going through the rest of the evening. We had a late dinner of MD's favorite tri-tip, rice, beans, corn tortillas, and veggies. I finished up the dishes and melted 6 liters of snow for our water in the morning and put it in the tent so it would not freeze overnight. We crawled into our cozy down sleeping bags and tried to sleep and get rested for the next day ahead.

The next morning was beautiful. I went and started cutting wood down for our fire and Tessa, Jan, and MD rebuilt our living area in style. We had hot chocolate and eggs and sausage with veggies for breakfast. After this was done, MD and I had a chance to do a Bible devotional which was a way to reflect on what God has done for us and how we can apply it to our lives now. It also opens for a deeper discussion and conversation that we might not have thought about as we have reflected on what we read. It strengthens our relationship.

By noon, we all decided to make a day trek to West Lake. We all put on our skis. I used my climbing skins on my skis for the first time and it sure helped make the hills easier to climb in the snow without sliding back. This was David's first time cross-country skiing and he did awesomely! So proud of him trying something new as he pushed through some difficult ascent and descents of the terrain. MD did great as well; it took a while to get him motivated, so talking about Legos was the key to getting him going. So, we talked about Legos and how my mom found some of my Legos as a kid and was going to give them to me which of course MD had no hesitation to suggest that he should have them.

Tessa and Jan were in their element and made skiing look graceful and full of finesse. Time was not on our side and we only made it to the ridge where the view of Red Mountain sat boldly in the distance sitting behind West Lake. It was quite a trek to get where we were and we did not want to be skiing back in the dark. So, we turned back to base camp. Once we got back we needed to get the fire going. MD tried, then Jan, and then Tessa, and then I stepped in and got it going. We made spaghetti and enjoyed our snow built living room with a toasty fire at our feet. We all went to bed to prepare for our last day in the Sierras.

Morning arrived and we had breakfast with hot chocolate. We packed up our gear and headed back to the car with our skis on. I was so impressed again with David and his ability to carry a loaded backpack with skis and balance so well. I am so proud of everyone who went. We covered a lot of ground, about 15 miles overall. Tessa broke out chips and salsa as we packed the van for a delicious treat and needed fuel for our bodies. Our final stop before home was our traditional spot, In-N-Out. It was so good!

To the team: I was impressed with Tessa's endurance, work ethics, and sense of humor. She is tough as an ox but compassionate and caring like a mother hen with her chicks. She always pushed me harder when it came to pulling the pulk sled up crazy terrain. I could not have done it without her.

I appreciated Jan's hard work and his passion for skiing. He also made me laugh with his innocence and sense of humor. You should hear him sing along with music in the car. No more shakes from In-N-Out for this kid.

I enjoyed David's free-spirited way of life. He was willing to try new things all at once, yet he never got frustrated and remained positive. I appreciated his asking us to take three minutes of silence to meditate each day, even on the trek up to base camp and stopping for three minutes to be still (that is hard for me because I want to keep going and "get 'er done"). The kids had no problem being still since they were so tired and could use that three minutes of rest and being still. I was able to reflect on God's Scripture in the Bible which says in Psalms, "Be still and know that I am God."

MD, I love you, my son. This, I think, was his hardest trek ever, as it was for me. He pushed through his typical high-altitude issues. I admire his leadership skills which are always evolving. His creativity, like his snow-cave-restroom with a window in it for all to enjoy. Although he is not an intense or competitive person like his dad, he still pushes himself beyond what he thinks he can do. I am truly proud of my son and his accomplishments. I love being his dad and watching him grow as a person. I am blessed.

It was so much fun and so beautiful. I am so sore and tired as I wrote this. I felt like I did a triathlon or half-marathon, pouring my heart into it. It was well worth the adventure, and I'm so thankful for this time away.

A Backpacking Trip Unlike My Wedding Day

February 2017

So, two weeks ago I was getting sick with a cold and trying everything to get better before another winter backpacking trip scheduled for February 16-20. The group joining me would be Andrew and two others, Kimberly and Roger. Then a week later, Kimberly got sick with a cold, too. This past week I was not looking any better but worse. I got some antibiotics on Wednesday the day before we were leaving. Then, Thursday morning, I woke up with a pink eye infection. I was determined to go, so I thought I could wear snow goggles the whole time so no one else would get infected and I would be on antibiotics. I was all good to go, right? NOT! I talked with Kimberly on Thursday morning to check on how she was feeling. She sounded horrible but maintained her bubbly, excited, energetic self.

My sweet wife and my wise father-in-law were also concerned because of a storm brewing in the Sierras. Well, I like this kind of stuff, it's more adventure and challenge. So, I just thought I would check the weather forecast from my friends at Huntington Lake where we were heading. Both told me it was the worst storm they'd had. "There is so much snow, unable to look at the view from the deck on the second floor because of the snow level, and there is a high chance of getting trapped in on the mountain when backpacking. Do not come up!" I was told.

Strike three! I am sick, Kim is sick, and it is too dangerous to be backpacking in the Western Sierras. I think God made it very clear that I should not go. So, I called Kim and she was relieved that we were not going. I called Roger while he was sitting at work counting the minutes to when he would head off to the mountains and told him the bad news. I felt so bad. He had packed all his gear in his car. He later told my wife that he would leave the gear in his car, except for his sleeping bag which needs to be hung, until March for another possible trip up there. I also had to break the news to Andrew and he was very sad, but asked if we could do another winter backpacking trip soon.

So, friends and family, I am recovering at home. I unpacked all the gear and then put it all away before the storm came through Thursday night and Friday. All I had to show from this trip are pictures of my vegetables before and after being dehydrated and my dehydrated fruit. I was able to give Kimberly and Roger the trail mix I made for them and the brownies that my wife made which were for the folks at the Tamarack Lodge, as it is tradition.

I am planning another trip in March and Roger is trying to figure out how to go. Kimberly is off to Hawaii in March, but we might try another trip in April. At this rate with these amazing storms, there should still be snow in April.

Until then, have a wonderful rest of your week. I will be just "hanging" around here resting and being with my bride at home. The photo from the beginning of this chapter has special meaning and significance. Do not attempt this at your wedding unless you are a climbing professional *and* cleared by your bride to do this. This photo was taken at our wedding. It was so much fun! I appreciate that Melody let me do this. The audience laughed and broke the nerves my bride and I were having. I came down in my cowboy tuxedo while *Mission Impossible* was playing in the background. The best day of my life!

S'mores Anyone? Winter Non-Sierras Trip

March 2017

It is a beautiful day in Goleta, 88 degrees this afternoon. This does not sound like the Sierras, right? Well, I injured my back at work nine days ago, spraining my thoracic and lumbar area, and I have not fully recovered yet. Thanks to the back brace, chiropractic work, and some rest from the hospital, I should heal much faster.

So, we had to cancel another winter Sierra trip. All of us were so disappointed, me, MD, Smiley Andy, and Roger Davids. It was meant to be. God has His reasons. I sure do not understand it, though. I will have to ask Him when I get to Heaven, along with the other questions I have. It is especially a bummer because I have been in such great health and training a lot to prepare for this trip and this summer as MD and I are going to do several triathlons together.

My boys are so gracious and understanding and so was Roger when I had to tell them. It was so hard to tell Andrew as he was bouncing off the walls with excitement the night before we were to leave and I had to break the news to him. So, I am trying to find fun things to do to make up for the trip. Lots of activities for us boys. Yesterday, I took Andrew to Martial Arts and MD had bike team practice. Afterward, we went to Pepe's Restaurant with Melody for dinner, and then I took Andrew to the gym and hung out in the jacuzzi while Andrew swam 400 yards in the pool, no joke. He has an amazing backstroke. We got home around 2145.

Today, my mom, "Nana," took the kids and their cousin, Paysen, to the movies and then played on the trampoline at her house. I took MD home and then rode our bikes to his swim lesson. MD's coach never showed up, so I volunteered and coached the kids swim team. It was fun. I love working with kids. We headed back home on our bikes to then pick up Andrew at Nana's house. We came home and MD made burritos for dinner all by himself. He is a great cook. Meanwhile, I set up the Kammok hammocks in the backyard to sleep in overnight. Before bedtime, the kids made s'mores and I supervised. Now it is bedtime, hoping the sugar rush has gone away so they can sleep.

More fun stuff tomorrow. Although we did not go to the Sierras, I have enjoyed spending time with my family here in Goleta. Melody (who was supposed to be getting a break from the high energy boys for these four days) is out with her friends tonight and tomorrow, so she is having some great bonding time with her girlfriends which is so needed.

MD loved his pajamas and said it was so appropriate for this "non-Winter Sierra camping trip." He was right. We are having "*snow much fun!*"

Well, this was an unusual backpacking trip to write up.

Just Chillin' - Father & Son Winter Backpacking Trip

April 20-23, 2017

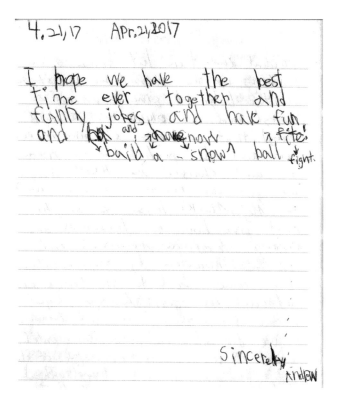

It was not a typical weekend for Andrew (six years old) and me. After school on Thursday, we drove up to the Western Sierras for his second winter backpacking trip. The theme throughout this trip was "Our God Provides." We were planning to sleep in our car once we got up there and be ready in the morning to head out. Well, my friend at a

Lodge up there where we park our car for the weekend said no way, you are our guest here, no charge. God provided. The brownies over these past sixteen years have paid off; the parking charge is usually fifty dollars. Thank you, Melody and Mom-in-law.

In the morning, Mayor Mark loaded our gear on his sled and we headed up to West Lake about 7.75 miles on the snowmobile. We stopped about a mile in to check our gear in the sled and one of my 3L water jugs broke and our gear was wet, however, our waterproof stuff sacks for our down sleeping bags were kept dry. I still had two 3L jugs intact. God provided.

We made it to West Lake in 45 minutes safely. We said our good-byes to our friend Mayor Mark and I gave him some gas money. I opened up our gear and found yellow fluid in my Bear Vault container and noticed that it originated from my egg container. We lost five out of six eggs. I guess the ride up here was a little bumpy. We used that one egg and some sausage for breakfast the next morning and we were satisfied. God provided.

After cleaning off the eggs from the rest of our food using the snow as my water source, we set up camp: our tent, kitchen area, and fire pit which was a dead tree which burned to the ground leaving a very large fire pit ring. I started digging out a snow cave but it became very clear that this was not going to work. So, I turned it into a purified water drip faucet system. The sun melted the snow at the entrance of the cave which filled up our water jugs. It was great. God provided. During the rest of the day, Andrew played in the snow, took two naps, and he tried to dig out the outhouse buried in the snow but it was too big of a task. I skied the surrounding area and on top of West Lake. Andrew and I played games in our tent because it was cold and windy. For dinner, we had tri-tip, veggies, beans, and rice. Before bed, we did our Bible devotional and read the Bible and both of us wrote in our journal. Andrew is really into it, too. We were in bed by 1800.

I could not sleep for the life of me. So, I got up at 0400 and explored the area and found at the end of the frozen lake running water, which I then used the broken water jug from the sled incident to collect water and bring it back to camp and boil it for ten minutes. More water to drink and use. Again, God provided. I made breakfast with that one egg, sausage, and hot chocolate to warm our bodies. Andrew and I ventured out into the vast forest and skied all over West Lake itself. Lots of fun. It has been a year since Andrew has cross country skied. I saw fresh coyote tracks and scat, but no bear sightings.

We played more board games, had a snowball fight, and built a very big snowman. That was so much fun. Andrew decided to get behind the snowman and pretend it was talking to me. We took a video of it. It was so funny! Andrew thought it was fun to hide a snowball in the snow and I had to find it. He is so hilarious. We had burritos for dinner. Again, before bedtime, we spent time in God's Word thanking Him for His provisions. We prayed and I even asked God to let me sleep tonight, and I had the best sleep I have ever had camping, seriously. God provided.

We decided in the morning to leave base camp and head back part of the way and camp closer to our car, just to break it up since it is a long trek back. We left West Lake at 0910, Andrew snowshoed and I skied with skins on the bottom of my skis which are awesome. Once the terrain was more flat and downhill, Andrew put on his skis. About 1.75 miles of 7.5 miles into our trek back, Andrew fell skiing and twisted his left knee really bad. He was crying and in lots of pain. If he is crying, then it is serious. I always say, he has no pain receptors. It takes a lot for him to express he has pain. His first comment to me was, "Dad, I wished you had a cell phone to call Mayor Mark to pick us up." I laughed inside, even if I had one, we probably could not get cell reception here. I assessed his knee and the only way to get out of here is to put him on my sled and pull the gear and him. I was scared and concerned. We stopped in our tracks and prayed that God would heal him and get us back to the car safely. So, I pulled him and the gear almost two miles when he said he wanted to try to ski. He got on his skis and said in a very loud voice, "God has healed me!"

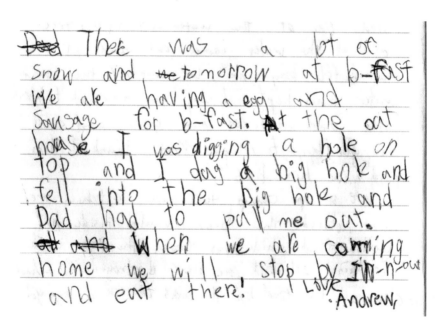

He and I skied, and at times he would ride the sled and I would pull him. As we got closer and closer to the car we were looking for a place to make camp for the night, but we agreed to head back to the car. We made it to the car in 6 hours 10 minutes, a very long day. Andrew's knee was really hurting but stable enough to drive home. We did stop in Kettleman City to eat at In-N-Out, I had to carry him because it hurt so bad. We arrived home last night safely and today we are going to see a doctor hoping he did not tear his ACL or any other ligaments or meniscus. His leg has an ace wrap and is resting today.

It was a wonderful trip. I am bummed we cut it a day short and that Andrew got injured. However, I really enjoyed being with my son and sharing this adventure. I enjoyed our daily devotions in God's Word and seeing first hand His provisions for us throughout the entire journey from the coast to the mountains and back. I loved seeing Andrew write in the journal and putting his thoughts down. It inspired me. He is an amazing kid. I am so proud of him. I am truly a blessed father.

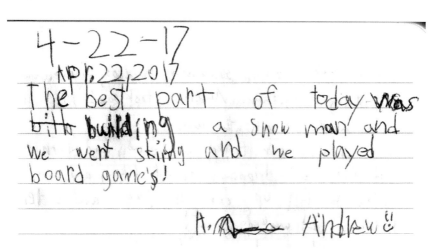

Santa Barbara Triathlon - A New Beginning

August 27, 2017

For the past couple of months Andrew (seven years old) and I have been training for the Santa Barbara Triathlon Sprint Course. It consists of a 500-yard ocean swim, 6-mile bike and a 2-mile run. Today was the day!

We got to East Beach at the Bath House at 0703. Our wave start was at 0830. It gave us enough time to set up our gear at the Transition Area and get out my jitters and butterflies in my stomach before the big race. When we showed up, my dad was there waiting for us. He lives in Thailand and was visiting for a month. I saw my very first triathlon when I was a boy, watching my dad compete in the Police Olympics Triathlon. This was a big deal for me to have my dad see my son and I compete.

As we set up our gear, my mom showed up and then my sister, Stephanie. Melody and MD were on their way after finding parking. Pricilla and Bill Lavorin from our church arrived as well. We headed to the Start line and were ready to race. Then one of my friends, Kim Siracuse from Santa Barbara Cottage Hospital who I had worked with on the cardiac floor was there, too. Melody's dad arrived. We had our cheering section. It was AWESOME!

The countdown began and we were off running into the water. Andrew had the biggest grin ever. The strong swimmers passed us by and we just plugged along. I was so proud of Andrew. I made deals with him; if he got to the next buoy before me, he would get a reward. First buoy, a 7-11 Slurpee, then second buoy Pepe's Restaurant on Tuesday night's buffet, third buoy, he got one hour on the computer. Well, he swam so well that he did the swim in 23:09. You could hear the cheers from the spectators on the beach and the life guards joined in as well. I was so moved by the overwhelming support from everyone.

We got out of the water, ran up the beach to the transition area and headed to where we'd prepared our bike and gear. We pulled the wetsuits off and got on our helmets and shoes and headed off on the bike course. He dominated on the bike, passing riders, pushing hard to make up some time since we were the last ones out of the water. His bike time was 33:48. Our training rides take us forty minutes to do six miles. He nailed it, averaging 10.4 miles/hr! I arrived at the transition area before him to get him ready for the run. He maneuvered through the transition area and found his bike rack/gear area perfectly. He knew exactly what to do and where to go. He was so focused.

We took our cycling shoes off and put on our running shoes, took our helmets off, strapped our bib number around our waist and headed out. He pushed through the pain in the legs and sore toes as he pounded on the pavement/ bike path. He passed some runners and then about 0.88 miles in he had to use the restroom. Me being slightly competitive, went in the bathroom with him, shouting, "Go Andrew. We have got to go before others catch up with us!"

We got back on the pavement and continued to run. We passed another runner, giving high-fives to runners coming back the other way and looking off to the distance, the turn around. We passed the water station, grabbed some water. Now, imagine trying to run fast while taking a drink. I laughed so hard as Andrew (he was laughing, too) was trying to take a drink and telling me, "Every time I take a drink I am shaking and the water just comes out and not in my mouth but on me and the ground."

We made the turn around spot and again through the water station and as I came through, all the high school girls volunteering at the water station had water cups filled to the brim and at the same time drenched me from both sides. It was so funny and Andrew was behind me laughing and then trying to get me wet with his water. We passed some more runners, cooled and refreshed. We both could see the finish line in sight as we approached the finish chute. Andrew was determined to beat me and I was determined to beat him. We both crossed the finish line, and Andrew appeared to have beat me by a toe length. He ran the 2 miles in 25:52, 12:21 min/mile pace (including the bathroom break).

Andrew and I finished the race in 1:31:37. I picked him up and cheered for the great accomplishment he had made. I was so proud of him for his training and his race. He is an amazing kid. Many times, he wanted to give up during our training days, but he had made a commitment to stick with it and race today. I love being his dad. He is awesome and I am so thankful to have had this opportunity to compete in this race with him.

Carpinteria Sprint Triathlon with Dad, MD, & Smiley Andy

September 24, 2017

I attempted to register online for the Carpinteria Triathlon for my two boys, but I could not enter Andrew online because he is only seven years old; too young I guess, although I didn't read an age limit. I also did not register myself because the cost would have been over $250.00 for all three of us, and I planned to just shadow Andrew along this course. I even signed a waiver and everything. Oh well.

At the event, a woman was injured prior to the race and came up to me and offered to give me her entry fee. I humbly and graciously accepted it which was definitely a gift from God. So blessed. So, I got all of us registered for the Sprint Triathlon (Sprint Course: 500-meter swim, 9-mile bike, and 3.1-mile run) and went home and got ready for our race the next day. It was so awesome to register MD (eleven years old) because this was his first triathlon. He really wanted to race after watching his brother compete at the SB Triathlon. MD only had one month to train because he had broken his arm over the summer. I was a bit nervous.

At 0610 in the morning, MD, Smiley Andy and I headed off to the Carpinteria Triathlon. MD and I had butterflies during the drive there while Andrew was cool and calm, since this was his second triathlon. Seriously, he was so cool! We found a great parking spot near the event and headed to the transition area to set up our gear. MD and Andrew racked their bikes up in the youth area while I had to go to my area to rack up my bike with the adults (although some would say I still act like a kid… my family, my church family, and some, well, a lot of my friends… okay, most). I came back to their bike rack area and helped set them up. My wife and my mom arrived to cheer us on. Once we got settled, we headed off to the swim start. MD asked if we could warm up in the ocean which was good thinking. We warmed up in the water then got out and stood in the corral of swimmers.

The countdown started and we were off in the ocean. MD took off like he had done it before and looked back several times to make sure we were okay. After passing the first buoy, I no longer saw MD. He was so fast. Andrew and I finally came out of the ocean in 30 minutes, greeted by cheering fans who were asking for Andrew's age. They were in awe that he was just seven. We arrived at the transition area and I stood at Andrew's side as he quickly transitioned into the bike stage. He headed off while I went to my bike rack area and transitioned to the bike portion of the race. I caught up with Andrew and we were off on the bike. Andrew dominated the hill climbs which he has worked so hard on in training. In the back of my mind I was wondering how MD was doing since he was long gone on the bike course.

We had about 1 mile left or so and were turning left onto Linden Ave. (Hwy 192/Foothill Rd/Casitas Pass Rd) at a three-way intersection with a CHP officer waving us to turn left. A female Olympic athlete on her bike was entering Linden Ave. from our right, which on the Olympic course needs to proceed through Linden Ave. to the State Beach where the race began. Andrew was coming to the intersection pretty fast and I looked to my right and saw this woman and was expecting to see her go straight, but she did not and turned left instead, which was the wrong way on the course, onto Hwy 192 toward us at a high speed.

Well, Andrew was already in the intersection turning left like he should and she plows right into him, knocking Andrew to the ground who took the brunt of the collision. I saw the whole thing in slow motion and there was nothing I could do. I rushed to Andrew so scared of what had happened. Andrew was in complete shock and calm, not like his dad who was so upset at the woman for running into my seven-year-old child.

For the past 8 miles during the whole bike course I was behind him to keep him safe from the cars behind me since there was not a bike lane for most of the course. I immediately brought Andrew and both of our bikes to the side of the road. Andrew had a laceration and abrasion to his left knee and found that his front wheel of his bike was bent and the frame and handlebars scratched up. I loosened the calipers/brakes to allow room for the wobble wheel to spin. Andrew got back on his bike and headed to the transition area while blood was dripping down his left leg and he was trying not to cry.

I was not sure if we could continue, especially on the run. We passed Melody and my mom near the transition area on our bikes but I did not give a heads-up to my wife with what had just occurred. As we approached the transition area, I called out to one of the Race Volunteers to grab one of their medical staff (which I have worked with at this event for six years) to meet us at Andrew's bike rack station. I put my bike at my bike rack and got transitioned to the run portion. I caught up with Andrew as he arrived at his bike rack. He wanted to continue! The medics came and I patched him up with their stuff and Andrew was ready to run, seriously, no question about it. It was game on.

Andrew ran like nothing had happened. I was still fuming so I was glad to run those emotions off. We were about a half-mile into the run and MD passed us as he was heading to the finish line. He had a great big smile and no sweat on his brow. He looked so strong. I could not believe he was this far in the race. Go MD! Suddenly, Andrew yelled out to me, "I have to go pee!" Not again… Remember the last race? Well, there is no place to go.

As we continued through the neighbors on the course, a woman was working in her garden in her front yard. I came up to her house and said, "Excuse me. My son and I are in the Carpinteria Triathlon and my son needs to go to the bathroom and we do not want to do it in someone's bushes." She was so sweet and let us use her bathroom in the house. We said our thanks and headed back on the course. Thank you God for the kindness she demonstrated towards us. Andrew kept running, trying to pick up the pace as we were running slower than our training runs. I also had to keep Andrew's injured left knee in consideration. About a half-mile left into the run he caught up to another runner and then passed her by. We could see the finish line and his eyes were set on the goal at hand. He got faster and faster and crossed the finish line just a second before me.

We had finished the race! I was so proud of him. MD was there to congratulate us on our victory finish. We all gave high fives. I told MD that I was so impressed with him and his accomplishment and racing his first triathlon. He said with confidence and excitement that he wanted to do the SB Triathlon and Goleta Beach Triathlon next year. He was so pumped. All three of us got medals for finishing. MD got fourth place in his age group. However, Andrew was called to the podium for a first place finish in his age group! He got two medals in one day. Melody, my mom, and I were so proud of both boys that day. I have some amazing young athletes. It is a true honor to see them race and to do it with them.

Introducing TRI Mountaineering: Winter Group Backpacking

February 15-18, 2018

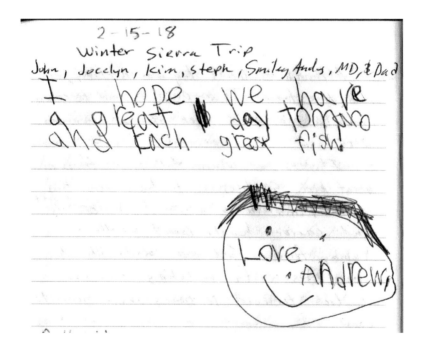

It is that time of the year again for winter backpacking trips. This trip was different. Last summer on a road trip to Colorado with my family, I was trying to think of a name for my winter trips. I came up with TRI Mountaineering. It was catchy… When I would share with people who were interested in going winter backpacking, I would tell them "Give it a TRI." Also, the TRI has a deeper meaning. TRI means three: Time, Teamwork, Transformation. Taking the Time away from your everyday life for a new way to reflect, meditate, rejuvenate, and reevaluate. Teamwork is important on a trip like this; everyone has to work together as one body, supporting and encouraging each other. A goal for me and everyone is to literally be Transformed, coming out of this trip as a better person and more balanced. I also use it to strengthen my relationship with God.

I had organized a wonderful group of people which included my sons, MD and Smiley Andy, my sister Stephanie, and Kim, John, and his wife, Jocelyn. The only experienced backpackers were myself and my boys, so we had lots of newbies on this trip. Although they were newbies, they were prepared and ready for the challenge. With the help of my mom and the entire team, we packed two cars by 1700 on Thursday evening and drove up to Tamarack Lodge near Huntington Lake and arrived around at 2230. I delivered my traditional cookies (thanks mom-in-law) and brownies (thanks John) to Daryl, the manager of the Lodge, and to Mayor Mark of Huntington Lake/Shaver Lake who has become a good friend and a huge help to me over the years. We finally laid our heads on pillows and fell asleep.

We woke up early the next morning and were met by Mayor Mark in the parking lot of the Tamarack Lodge with his off-road vehicle who said he would take us up to the locked gate about two miles from West Lake. Awesome! It was about 7.75 miles to West Lake from the Lodge. The trail had deep snow and dirt making the trip a slight challenge for me. I had recently injured/torn my left shoulder which may require rotator cuff surgery (the MRI results look bad) and I'm meeting with a surgeon this week. I brought my pulk sled and a Burley Nomad bike trailer with poles attached to it to pull my gear on the dirt. Due to my shoulder, I could not carry my gear on my backpack. I brought both up because the terrain required both. It was going to be a challenge, but I was so thankful we had both. They helped out a lot.

So, we loaded up the gear on the off-road vehicle and Andrew and I got in. Around 0900, Mayor Mark drove us up as far as we could through deep powder snow and dirt reaching the locked gate. We unloaded our gear and Andrew and I headed to West Lake. Mayor

Mark drove back to pick up three more from our team. Andrew and I stopped about a mile or so to wait for everyone.

The next part of the hike was maneuvering through dense forest, off the trail so we did not lose anyone. We waited and waited and waited and no one showed up. We waited over an hour. It should only have taken forty minutes to go back and come to the locked gate and then hike to where we were, and I was getting a bit nervous. I told Andrew to stay put and I hiked back to the locked gate to see if anyone was there. Well, no one was there. I was really worried. I hiked back to Andrew and told him that we should wait until 1200. I was concerned that maybe Mayor Mark crashed his vehicle or something happened to the Team on the way up.

So, with wisdom from God, we decided to head back to the Lodge which meant pulling the pulk sled through snow and dirt/rocks. We pushed through about 2.5 miles back when a voice came on our hand-held radio. It was John. I was so relieved! He said, "Hang tight there and we will be joining you soon." He explained that Mayor Mark crashed his off-road vehicle on the way back to the Lodge and walked back to his house. He actually passed three of the team members on the trail because they were concerned something had happened to us since Mayor Mark had not arrived to pick them up. They had decided to hike in just in case something was wrong, kind of like a search Team.

Mayor Mark went home, got his truck with chains, and picked up the rest of the team and met us near the locked gate. John and Kim then went back with Mayor Mark to the broken off-road vehicle and loaded it onto the truck. Mayor Mark drove back to his house leaving John and Kim to catch up with the rest of the team. We were then all joined together and headed to West Lake. We finally made it to West Lake and found the spot where Andrew and I had camped last year; a perfect location. It was awesome!

West Lake was so beautiful. The lake was frozen over, snow was on the mountain, and patches of snow were at our campsite. As a team we set up our six-man tent leaving me sleeping in my Kammok hammock nearby. If you were not setting up the tent and inflating the sleeping pads, you were starting the fire. MD, Stephanie, and John together started the fire with flint and steel. It was amazing to watch from a distance how everything flowed well together. So proud of the team already. Once settled in, we had a lovely tri-tip dinner which everyone enjoyed. There were lots of laughs and reflecting on the time spent on the hike into West Lake, being grateful that everyone was safe. I truly think that the time spent on the start of this adventure brought everyone closer together as a team. The transformation was already in progress.

The next morning, we gathered together to have eggs and sausage for breakfast. Since the lake was frozen over, the team decided to try ice fishing for the first time. It was fun to see everyone involved in making their own ice hole. No one caught a fish, but the smile on their faces never left them. It was a wonderful afternoon.

After fishing, Kim and Andrew went exploring. Andrew loved hanging with Kim. She is a bundle of energy, a ray of sunshine and so sweet to my kids. John and I had a chance to hang out together and explore as well. We were crossing a meadow and I jumped over the water but the sides gave in and both of my boots were in the water, soaked. I was so thankful that I had brought my trail running shoes which remained on my feet for the rest of the trip while my boots continued to dry, even now as they sit on a table outside drying out. Stephanie and Jocelyn had some opportunities to talk and build a friendship. It was a great day.

That night we made some burritos and sat around the campfire sharing our thoughts and reflecting on what the trip meant to each one of us. Steph got a migraine and tried to sleep in her sleeping bag but she was so uncomfortable. I offered some nursing and brotherly love and she finally fell asleep. The rest of the team discussed leaving on Sunday because of the concern of a storm coming in on Sunday night. We agreed as a team to head out Sunday. We all did a Devotional and Kim read some Scripture. Jocelyn spoke about prayer and her challenge of staying focused while talking with God.

Sunday morning, we made pancakes and warmed our bodies by the fire. Steph said she felt better and I was so thankful. Kim shared with us about her nightmare. Then we all pitched in and packed up our gear. We headed out at 1100 and hiked back to the car. It was tough! No one complained, not even my boys. The trail was difficult at times as we navigated through thick woods, deep snow, and the weather was changing as we got closer to our car. The wind picked up and temperatures got colder. We had hiked back to our car in less than four hours. We were all so tired and still had the drive home. Stephanie, Andrew, John, and Jocelyn drove in one car and Kim drove with me and MD. Stephanie was determined to get home, and she did, about twenty minutes before us. We all enjoyed eating at our traditional In-N-Out on the way home, too.

I think all of us needed to take time away and be in the presence of God's creation. I was in awe of the teamwork that everyone showed. They are all wonderful, caring, hardworking individuals. I was truly blessed by them. It was also an amazing, challenging, fun, and transforming trip. I know that that trip will leave an impression on my heart as well as those that came.

I appreciate John's patience and humble servant-like attitude and for bonding with my boys. I am grateful for Jocelyn and her quiet, behind-the-scenes nature, and getting things done and for her willingness to share from the heart to strangers who became friends. My little, but much taller sister, Stephanie for her courage and ability to conquer her fears, pain, and challenges. To be away from her kids I know was so hard. I am very proud of what she accomplished this weekend and thanks for watching out for my kids, too. As for Kim, you can babysit my kids anytime. My kids adore her. She is always positive, and her laugh could be heard from afar. MD asked me, "How can anyone be so happy for so long on a trip, non-stop happy?" MD was the king of fire. He made sure the fire was always going. Andrew, what can I say? You are Smiley Andy. You are so funny. It is agreed by the team that he should be a comedian. He makes everyone laugh.

Thank you for reading my "novel" as my dad calls it. It means a lot and I hope it excites you and helps you reflect about you and your family. Thank you Stephanie, Kim, John, and Jocelyn and my boys for going on this incredible trip. Friends for life.

Facing the Storm Head On
- Winter Sierra Trip

March 23-26, 2018

Winter Sierra Backpacking Trip
Smiley Andy and Dad   3-23-18
Hope me have a great day tomorrow.

This day has been good.

We are sleeping at May or marks house and we ate dinner.

LOVE,
Andrew

The theme of this adventure with Smiley Andy is "Facing the Storm Head On!" On Friday morning, thanks to my wonderful co-worker Sally M., I was able to leave at 1000 which gave me enough time to pack and load the car, pick up my son from school and pick up the wonderful and yummy chocolate chip cookies from my mother-in-law's house. Off we went at 1300.

We made good time to the Huntington Lake area in the Western Sierras and there was snow everywhere. We were invited to stay the night at our friend, Mayor Mark's house. I made sure Mayor Mark got some of those delicious cookies and also Daryl, the manager of the Tamarack Lodge down the street—a standard tradition when we go up there. Mayor Mark said since there was still daylight, he brought out two snowmobiles for us to ride together. I left Andrew behind with his wife, Jillian, in their house. We headed off into the wilderness and it was absolutely breathtaking. It was so much fun riding a snowmobile alone for the first time. It looks easy but there is a learning curve for sure. He brought me to a spot on the mountain that overlooked a canyon to see the spectacular mountain range on the other side. The sun was setting so the colors of the mountain range were beautiful. We made our way back to the house and had a wonderful dinner. We said our good nights and headed to bed. Andrew and I laid in bed and did our Bible Devotional and then some journal writing. After that, we were asleep.

The next morning, we woke up to some delicious egg burritos to warm our bellies. Mayor Mark offered to load our gear into a sled and pull us on his snowmobile. So, all three of us loaded onto one snowmobile and headed off to our basecamp around 5.5-6 miles away. On the way there, I somehow lost my balance over a snow bump and fell off the snowmobile and rolled behind them avoiding the sled behind the snowmobile. I was ok, but it rattled me a bit.

We finally reached our destination, the spot where MD, Ben and I had camped at years ago, and said our goodbyes. The view was spectacular. Off in the distance were some dark, ugly clouds headed our way. I knew we needed to prepare for this storm. So I set up our tent and built snow blocks near the entryway to prevent snow from blowing in. Andrew tried to start the fire with flint and dryer lint, but let me do it after a while. We finally got the fire going, then I made the kitchen area with a Kammok shelter above it and snow blocks to prevent wind and snow from coming into our kitchen area. We ate lunch and then we decided to try to build an igloo, but it was way too difficult (unlike the YouTube videos that made it look easy), so we worked on a snow cave but hit a big rock. The depth of the snow was only about five feet or less so making a snow cave would have been challenging anyway. Oh, well.

Mayor Mark and two of his friends came by on snowmobiles to check on us. His two friends Larry and Mike thought the basecamp looked awesome and stood by the tent for some pictures. I thought it was so funny. I felt like they were tourists and never seen anything like this. Mayor Mark explained to them that we really like doing this crazy stuff. They said their goodbyes and headed off to Red Mountain.

About an hour later, the storm had moved into our area and the temperatures dropped and it really started to snow, sideways due to the increased winds. We made our way into our kitchen area and made dinner of tri-tip, beans, rice, and veggies. It was so good! After dinner, we did the dishes, made hot water for our Nalgene bottles which went into one-gallon Ziploc bags to put into our sleeping bags to make them nice and warm to get into later. We finally crawled into our sleeping bags in our tent, had our Bible devotional, some journal writing, then a game of checkers. Andrew loves playing games. We finally closed our eyes and went to sleep. During the night I could hear the snow pounding our tent. Although we were out here alone,

I knew we were protected by God's hands. He really sheltered us in this storm.

By morning, our tent was partially covered, although we might have had more if I had not shaken the tent to get the snow off periodically. The temperature in our tent said 15 degrees. I was not sure I wanted to get out of my sleeping bag. But we were hungry, so I made breakfast and brought it to Andrew since the weather was not in our favor. Finally, the storm let up and by afternoon we got to play outside and ski on some of the nearby hills. Andrew was amazing. This was his third time skiing on cross country skis and he did awesome and had so much fun. I had new skis and expected to just take off with ease, but flew out of them! Nothing broken but my pride. Once we made it down the hills, we needed to climb back up, so we put our climbing skins on the bottom of our skis and climbed up the hills. It worked perfectly, gripping the snow, preventing us from sliding backwards. After a day of skiing, we made our snowman at basecamp and played a game of backgammon and chess. That was fun.

We made spaghetti for dinner. While eating dinner, Andrew, with his wisdom, wanted to leave in the morning and felt that if another storm hit on Tuesday, that it might be difficult to get out. So, we prepared to leave. I am so thankful for Andrew and that I listened to him because on Monday afternoon, the weather started to turn stormy. God whispers in the ears of a child, be prepared to listen. After cleaning up dinner, Andrew went to bed. I stayed up to boil water for the Nalgene bottles for our sleeping bags, but I could not get the stove to work. I took it apart four times before I could get it going.

It was a pretty good night after I figured out how to stay warm. What I did was to cinch the head of the sleeping bag tight so only my mouth was sticking out for air. We woke up to beautiful skies. We spent some time in our tent having breakfast and playing a game of chess. We did our Bible Devotional and prayed for a safe trip back to our car. We gathered our gear and packed up and finally left by 1130.

On the way back, we were greeted by Mayor Mark on his snow-mobile, making sure we were okay. I felt like God was watching out for us. I was so impressed with Andrew's skiing. He would take a route on the descents that I would have walked down. He was looking more comfortable on these skis. He was ahead of me most of the time. However, our journey back to the car was an experience I would rather not do again. My precious Andrew had something happen to him but he has asked me not to disclose and is okay with what I have written. I will say, God did provide though. God supplied me with what I needed to help my son. I felt so bad for him. He handled it really well, and so did I. After four grueling hours, we finally made it back to the car. We stopped by Mayor Mark's house to get cleaned up.

We were on the road around 1645. We stopped at our traditional In-N-Out. The drive back was long but smooth. I was really tired after a long day of packing up the gear, skiing, and then driving home. We made it home safely, arriving around 2200. Melody was surprised to see us back so soon, but thankful we made it back and had a wonderful trip.

It was a perfect storm. The storm brought my son and I closer together as we bonded in the tent or our kitchen over meals, Bible Devotionals, board games, and just chillin' in our sleeping bags. The storm brought us fresh powder to ski on and a clear and beautiful day. In the storm, a friend checked on us to make sure we were safe, God's angel. That has never happened to me before in all my years of doing winter backpacking. In the storm, God gave us what we needed, not more or not less. It is a trip I will never forget. I will say again, I love being a dad. I love the relationship that I have with my kids. There is nothing like bonding with your child in the mountains without all the distractions of everyday life.

Thanks for sharing this journey with me as you read this. I hope it inspires you and encourages you to get out there and explore with the ones you love.

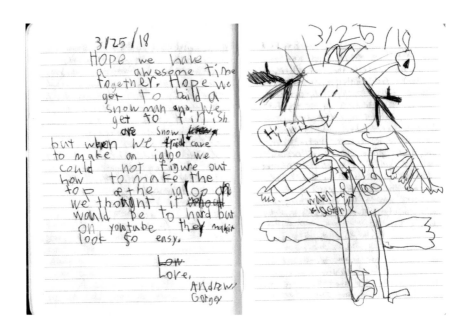

3/25/18

Hope we have a awesome time together. Hope we get to build a snowman and we get to finish our snow ~~fort~~ but when we tried our to make an igloo we could not figure out how to make the top of the igloo we thought it ~~would~~ would be to hard but on youtube they makin look so easy.

~~Lov~~
Love,
Andrew
George

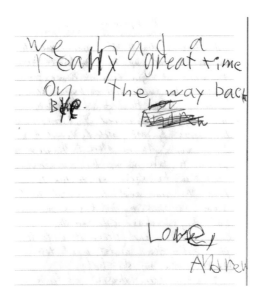

we really had a great time on the way back ~~Bye~~. ~~Love Andrew~~

Love,
Andrew

Catalina Island Marine Institute

April 16-20, 2018

I had the most wonderful opportunity to join MD with his Sixth grade class from Brandon School this past week to CIMI (Catalina Island Marine Institute), an awesome sixth grade science camp. We loaded up on the SB Airbus from the school very early at 0515 and made our way down to Long Beach. Then we traveled by boat to Toyon Bay, Catalina Island. There were a lot of sick kids and the boat crew were vigilantly hosing the side of the boat as we traveled two hours across the Pacific Ocean. We arrived with cheering and screaming by the students as well as the staff at the camp. We settled in the dorms and thank goodness for having the chaperones in their own rooms to themselves. The boys are messy and the aroma of their rooms together... you get the picture.

There were so many activities from rock climbing, sunrise hikes, night hikes with astronomy teaching, day hikes learning plants, hands-on marine education with cool aquariums to look and touch what was inside like sharks and crabs. We looked through microscopes to see creatures at the micro level. We kayaked, snorkeled, played fun beach and land games, and the kids played their favorite free time game in the "Gaga Pit", a derivative of dodgeball. We even got to go inside the belly of a whale. The kids got to dissect a squid, which MD was not so fond of. The teachers there were so knowledgeable and passionate about what they were teaching. The food was great, too! Seriously.

It was hard to leave Friday, not just because of Mike, the Bison who hung out at camp a lot of the time and this time by the luggage. It was an amazing place with so much learning that I could not contain it in my brain. It was so beautiful. One of my favorite parts was leading a group of 25 kids at 0600 on an amazing hike to the "Shrine" look out at the top of a mountain ridge overlooking the ocean and watching the sunrise. I had the kids be silent for two minutes, to take in this moment and to reflect, listen, and to be still. Ten minutes went by and they were still taking in the beauty of their surroundings without talking or making any noise. It was awesome! All I could do under my breath was to thank God for His wonderful, spectacular creation and to "be still and know that He is God."

One of my goals was to finish a book I had been reading, *Mud, Sweat, and Tears* by Bear Grylls, before the 28th of April (that's another novel in itself). I have been reading this book since last Father's Day. It is only 401 pages. I had 225 pages left. I do not like to read because it is a challenge for me. I have dyslexia and a learning disability. It is really hard to stay focused, I get bored and I drift off in my mind to something else. I would rather go for a run or even clean the bathroom. Each night at camp, in my bunkbed before I closed my eyes to go to sleep, I would spend about thirty minutes to an hour reading this book. Well, five minutes on the bus heading back to Goleta from Long Beach, I finished it! I actually cheered on the bus. No one really cared or knew why I was so happy. It was a huge accomplishment for me. What I took from this book was to get out there and experience life to the fullest. When you fall down, get back up and give it your best. I saw these kids for their very first-time hike, kayak, snorkel, touch a shark or sea urchin, have a lobster put on their head, tasted or smelled an edible plant, navigate by the stars above, rock climb, jump off the deck of the pier or do long division. Some were scared, unsure of themselves, worried about what others thought, afraid, but they all tried. Some failed but they tried again. They never gave up. They found joy in something new for their very first time.

CIMI is a spectacular place, one of a kind. Although CIMI stands for Catalina Island Marine Institute, it also could mean, "CIMI (SEE ME) as I am now." I think it changed all of us at this place.

Bear Grylls Survival Challenge

April 28, 2018

Mission accomplished April 28th, 2018! My sister, Stephanie, and I just got back from the Bear Grylls Survival Challenge in Santa Clarita, CA. Bear Grylls is from England and was with Her Majesty's Special Forces, a chief Boy Scout, and climbed Mt. Everest at age twenty-three and is also known for his TV show, *Man vs Wild*. The Bear Grylls Survival Challenge was brought to the U.S.A. for the first time today. It was a four-mile course with 18 survival challenges, 5 survival skills, 2 mountain climbs, one called Mount Everest. It was a very physical and very mental race.

Before the race, I had the privilege to be interviewed by a movie crew. Only a few were chosen and I was one. That was so cool. They said it will probably be accessed through social media and maybe on TV.

At 1000, about 30-50 competitors were in a closed metal room and then with a BOOM, the challenge began. First, we had to climb a mountain which was so grueling. It was so hot. Some of the other challenges were entering a "Middle Eastern city" and had to navigate while there were military personnel shooting weapons, lots of chaos to see if we could handle the situation. We maneuvered through a pitch-black cave, had to throw a spear and pierce a target, shoot a weapon and hit a target, and jump into four feet of water while trudging through an obstacle course. We had to carry sand bags while climbing over hay bales, drag a 100-150-pound punching bag around a Huey helicopter, eat crickets (MD and my nephew ate one), start a fire with flint, and solve a maze using a compass with clues… all this while running and climbing up mountains in between. It was so much fun, hard and exhilarating. After it was over, I really wanted to do it again. I could not believe it was all over. We had been training for five or six months.

After the race, I did a follow up with the movie crew. I am looking forward to seeing what comes out of that. What a wonderful and rare opportunity to do that.

One of the best parts of this day, besides racing this extreme event with my wonderful, younger sister, Stephanie, was at the end of the event, I got to meet Bear Grylls who was sitting in the passenger seat of a black SUV. My sister stood in front of the car with her arm raised up in a "STOP" motion. The car stopped and Bear rolled down the window and I was right there. Awesome! I got to shake his hand and say thank you. I also made something for him to show how much he has influenced my life as well as my kids.

I want to say thank you for all the support from our family and friends (my mom, my bride, MD, Smiley Andy, my sister's kids Paysen and Madisen, our godmother Kary, and Marc, Shellbell, and Michaela Hutcheson and Jen and Geoff Gilbert who let Stephanie and I stay at their house the night before). It was wonderful to hear your voices cheering us on in the distance. I am so glad that they were there. It was a long day for them, too. My sister and I are so blessed!

What a great day!

Ski to Sea

May 27, 2018

This past weekend I had a wonderful opportunity to race the Ski to Sea in Bellingham, Washington. It consisted of cross country skiing on Mount Baker, then downhill skiing/snowboarding, running, road biking, canoeing, cyclocross, and the final leg kayaking in the ocean, a total of 94 miles. I was invited by Backcountry.com (a sponsor for this race), the best backpacking/gear store located in Park City, Utah. They compete in an eight-man relay team in the Ski to Sea and on that team, they choose a customer to compete with them. I received an email from Colleen at Backcountry several weeks ago asking if my wife and I would like to be on their team. Melody and I decided that I should go since this was not her thing. So, Backcountry took care of me from transportation, lodging, food, entry fee, and the demo bike to use on the cyclocross leg. I was so appreciative of what they did for me. I was so blessed!

On a side note, several weeks earlier we received a bouquet of beautiful flowers from Backcountry as a way to show love and kindness over the loss of one of MD's friends who had passed away just recently. They are truly a rare company who go above and beyond for their customers. They genuinely care about their customers and to me it seems that these relationships are one of their goals in running their business.

On Friday, I flew from Santa Barbara, CA to Bellingham, WA. It was a smooth flight. I was picked up by Colleen and Ashleigh (one of the Backcountry Gearhead athletes) then driven to the hotel and we picked up the rest of the team to go to the Ski to Sea Party. It was a blast. Great music, awesome food, and great fellowship with my new teammates.

The next day, we ran some errands and then they dropped me and my demo Alchemy Atlas road bike off at the cyclocross leg start. I spent an hour riding through the course, learning the trails and roads and getting used to the bike. Later that evening, we went out to dinner and hung out with the team. We all needed our rest as race day was tomorrow, so we headed back to the hotel to go to bed.

It was race day! Half the team left at 0445 while some of us left at 0900. Fitz (our awesome bike mechanic) and I went to the cyclocross leg at 0900 to set up and provide assistance to the cyclists and as they came in droves to get their tire pressures checked, change flats, adjust their gears, and most of all give them encouragement as they were about to compete in this incredible race ahead of them. It was a lot of fun for me because I was able to help in the bike tent with some of the knowledge that I have about bikes. The best part of this was that after I had finished my leg of the race, athletes would come to me and share their story about their race and how much they appreciated Backcountry's help on fixing their bike.

It was now 1530, and my canoeist teammates arrived (placing first in their division leg) and I took the time chip wristband from them and put it into my Santa Barbara Triathlon Club tri-suit pocket. I got on my bike and headed through the obstacles and barriers along the course. After a minute on the course I lost my water bottle, but I kept riding. It was a very hot and dry day. It was a very difficult, challenging course with a fast pace. As I pounded swiftly and hard with my legs around and around the crank, I could hear the panting coming from my mouth and feel my heart pumping vigorously while looking at my Garmin 920 heart rate monitor as it showed my heart rate going 180+ beats per minute.

I tried to pace myself as I had 13+ miles of this intense course with this heat and with no water. I was passed by some riders zipping along the way and managed to pass some as well. At one point, I saw some riders far ahead so I pushed even harder and caught up with them. Then I noticed it was just a father and son going for an afternoon ride and not in the race. I just laughed as I passed them by. After 54 minutes, I crossed the finish line of this leg, even had to fight to cross the finish line as I was side by side with another rider. That was the best part. I love that about pushing to the finish line while neck and neck with another competitor. I was later picked up and we headed down to the finish line to meet the rest of the team.

We ended up placing fifth overall in the Recreational Mixed Division (53 teams). We were so happy. The team celebrated next to a really good food cart and next to it was a place where you could bring your dog to play with other dogs and drink beer or whatever. It was a cool idea. It was fun to watch the dogs chase each other while we relaxed while eating our burritos. We were all beat, so we headed back to the hotel after.

The next morning the Backcountry folks headed back to Utah while I ate breakfast at the hotel with some of the people who were involved with the race. It was a great time! I had so much fun. By 0930, I was on a plane heading back to Santa Barbara.

I am so thankful I had this opportunity to compete in this race. I appreciated getting to know the Backcountry Gearheads individually. They are all wonderful and totally awesome. I have so much respect for them.

The Little Engine That Could - 65 Mile Carp Bike Trek

June 30 - July 1, 2018

While MD and my wife, Melody, went to an exciting Dodgers base-ball game with a bunch of Dodger fans from church, Andrew and I decided to go on a 65.40-mile, round-trip bike trek to Carpinteria State Beach from our house where we camped at the hike and bike. Andrew did a great job and never gave up. He never complained, unlike me as I was pulling the bike trailer riding a 29" mountain bike. He was absolutely amazing. When we arrived at camp, Andrew never stopped moving. He is the energizer bunny on steroids. He played at the park and at the beach, buried in the sand three times and played in the ocean, then back at the park, then dinner at The Palms, then back playing at the park. You would think he did not even ride his bike 33.18 miles in 3 hours 40 minutes (including one stop at 7-11 for a Slurpee). We finally went to bed around 1900. We needed our rest, because we were back on the saddle the next morning.

Morning arrived way too quickly. We packed up and went to Esau's for breakfast. We made a pit stop at the park one more time for Andrew. Then we headed back to Goleta, once again Andrew and his unending endurance made it back safely and made great time, 32.22 miles in just over 3 hours 43 minutes. I hope he keeps this up, so he can ride on the local Echelon bike team, then a high school team and in college… then ride in the Tour de France. He is such a natural. His ability to climb hills is crazy. He is really King of the Mountains! Once again, so blessed to have this bonding time with my son. So important.

Dreams In the Making -
Goleta Beach Triathlon

July 29, 2018

On your Mark, get Set, GO! Today MD ran his second triathlon, but his first at the Goleta Beach Sprint Triathlon. It was a family event. We had Melody the photographer, Smiley Andy as a volunteer at the finish line who also handed out the prizes at the podium, and Dad as the coach and volunteer at the Finish Line. It was a beautiful and calm day at Goleta Beach. The ocean water was almost still, the bike course was fast, and the run was the place to catch up with your eyes on the finish line.

I was a proud dad, but I paced a lot as I watched MD race. I do not know how my wife, Melody, and my mom can stand still in one place and be so calm.

At the start while walking to the starting line, MD had pulled a muscle in his right leg. Not a great way to start the day. His swim was slow, but steady. His leg was really hurting out in the water as he tried to kick through the turbulence as other athletes passed him by. He never gave up. I paced back and forth along the beach, concerned for MD as I could see him slowly progress through the water with every stroke. I wanted to be right there with him to encourage and motivate him, but he wanted to do this on his own. He finally came out of the water and some peace came over me.

He ran along the beach to the transition area with his brother alongside him, cheering him on. He arrived at transition and calmly put on his bike gear. He headed out on his bike. I knew he would do really well on the bike. I "loaned" him my P2C Cervelo bike and boy did he look good! While on the bike course, I was able to get on my own bike and ride out onto the course where I could take pictures of him and encourage him that his dad was nearby to support him. He made it back to transition and switched to run mode and off he went. His pain in the right leg was non-stop on the course, but he was driven to finish the race and finish strong. His brother again came alongside him to motivate him to finish well. He crossed the finish line in 1 hour 47 minutes. Not only did he finish, but medaled by placing third in his age group. So proud of him.

What a day! MD, great job, my son. I love you! It was another proud day for the George family. He said he really enjoyed the race. He tried so hard he even has very large blisters on his big toe to prove it. Carpinteria Triathlon is in September and I hope both boys do it again. It was a fun day for all of us.

The Three Amigos - Lompoc Junior Triathlon

August 4, 2018

After last Sunday's triathlon with MD, there was another one in Lompoc, California, called the Lompoc Junior Triathlon. So, this morning, my family and I got in the car, picked up our friends, Jill and her son, Stosi, and headed north to Lompoc. What is in Lompoc? I have asked myself that many times. Well, there is Jalama Beach, which supposedly has the best hamburgers, but that was not where we were going.

Days leading to the triathlon, Stosi was interested in competing with my boys. Stosi had never done one before. He is an incredible cyclist and rides for a local cycling team. So, I prepared a race kit for him and had him borrow MD's bike. We did a training swim in the gym pool and on Friday, the day before the race, he came over and practiced a mini triathlon with my boys so he felt comfortable on race day. Now have The Three Amigos, Stosi, MD, and Smiley Andy competing.

When we arrived, we unloaded the bikes and unpacked all our gear at the transition area. I asked Stosi if he had everything on the checklist that I gave him the night before. He looked in his bag and his helmet was missing. We were one hour away from home and only forty-five minutes until the start of the race. Imagine the stress and frustration. MD, Smiley Andy, and Stosi got together and brainstormed ideas to make it possible for Stosi to race. Since Andrew's race was shorter in his division, they thought when Andrew got back from his bike, Stosi could then use his helmet. This was a wonderful idea and well thought out. For Stosi, medaling on the podium was not his focus; he just wanted to complete the race.

The race started in the Aquatic Center's pool where Smiley Andy and his division had to swim 50 yards, bike one mile, then run a quarter-mile. MD and Stosi had to swim 100 yards, bike two miles, then run a half-mile in their division. They all started at the same time. It was a very fast paced race.

The whistle blew and off they went, everyone giving their best. The energy behind the power of the swimmer's kick and stroke echoed in the facility. Smiley Andy did great, but was second to last place on the swim, but made up incredible time on the bike, passing every cyclist. He was amazing. He made it to transition and quickly was on the run. There was nobody behind him that you could see on the run, leaving them in the dust. He finished the triathlon and was in first place!

MD was awesome on the swim, holding his position of fourth place. Quick transition on the bike where he shined the most. He breezed through the bike course passing every rider. He kept the lead at transition and continued to hold his position on the run. There was another boy in his age group closing the gap, but it was over. MD finished first and placed first overall! It was so awesome!

Stosi was incredible for having this being his first race. He was second out of the water, but then had to wait in the transition area for Andrew to return back from the bike portion. As he waited and waited calmly, an athlete that had finished the Sprint Triathlon an hour earlier asked him if he wanted to borrow his helmet. Stosi did not hesitate and put on the helmet and took off on his bike. He managed to pass several riders as he desperately wanted a medal. He made it back to transition and took off running. He was in such a hurry that half his left foot was out of his shoe, his heel was on top of the back of the shoe. He crossed the finish line and without his knowledge, finished the race in third place. MD, Smiley Andy, and I congratulated him for his success and amazing performance.

I could not believe it. Both of my boys placed first and Stosi placed third. It was an exciting day! The awards ceremony was great, too. MD honored his brother for finishing first. Even the announcer recognized the loudest spectator and his contribution to the race… MD and Smiley Andy's dad, which would be me. I cannot help it, it is in my blood. I get so involved and excited. I hope I can learn to minimize my coaching during their races and let them be on their own. Every video I take, there is my loud and enthusiastic voice cheering them on and guiding them during the race. My wife says, "It is not necessarily a bad thing, unless you are watching them on videos, like on Facebook."

Even though this race was much shorter than the races that MD and Smiley Andy have done in the past, competing in Sprint Triathlons (500m swim, 15k bike, 5k run), this was much more of a chill and fun race, but still competitive. It was also a wonderful morning to hang out with my family and friends.

What's next, maybe the Carpinteria Triathlon at the end of September? It is so much fun to watch. These kids are getting the taste of victory and fun competition.

Anniversary, Family, & Friends - Camping & White Water Rafting

American River, Lake Tahoe, and Reno

August 12-18, 2018

This was an amazing trip with my family to see friends and go camping and white-water rafting on the American River, camp at Lake Tahoe, and Reno.

Our journey began as we headed up north to Visalia to see an old friend of mine from back in the days when I was working as a climbing director and ropes course instructor at Mount Herman Christian Camps in 1997. One of my staff was Ryan Corum who was passionate about the outdoors. I taught him everything I knew about climbing. We even ventured out into the local mountains of Santa Cruz, Idyllwild, and even in my hometown of Santa Barbara. He thrives on adventure and is a gear junkie like his teacher. He is a Visalia Deputy Sheriff and works for the Search and Rescue Team. I was very humbled when he shared with me that he chose that profession because of me sharing my love for the outdoors with him. He even got me a Search and Rescue shirt from his department that states, "Your worst nightmare is our vacation." I am so proud of what he has become and that he carries that passion like I do. It was a wonderful time to be with Ryan and his family and reflect on our memories together and the ones we want to create in the future.

The funny thing about Mount Herman is that is where my love and friendship began with my wife. What was also so cool about this particular trip was that the next day in Visalia was August 12, which was our eighteenth anniversary. We had to celebrate our marriage somehow! So, I took crayons and paper and made signs that said, "Just Married, 18 Years Ago!" and put them in our car windows so we could share our excitement of being married. I also cut out a heart with red construction paper and wrote some sappy love things about her and gave it to her when she woke up that morning.

As we left Ryan's house, Andrew woke up on the wrong side of the bed, actually, the wrong side of our solar system. Now parents, I learned something about consequences and road trips. Choose a consequence that will not have an effect on the rest of the family that are in the car. For example, taking away electronics as a consequence. I think Melody and I suffered the most. He did everything in his power for four hours to irritate, make loud noises, throw things, and so forth. I was ready to get out of the car and grab the bike off the bike rack and ride to our destination. Another thought occurred in my head as well. I know what you're thinking… I was going to take the child out of the car and put him on the side of the road with the sign "Help, I need to catch up with my loving family." Any suggestions for what to do with a cranky kid?

We finally arrived at our destination at Camp Lotus, in Coloma. We set up camp, jumped in the river and relaxed. Once we settled in for the night, we went to bed. MD and I slept in our Kammok hammocks, and Melody and Andrew were in the Marmot Halo 6 tent. The next morning, we ate breakfast and hung out at the river. Andrew took out my Nemo Cosmo Insulated Pad and traveled down the river. He was having so much fun, he even went through some rapids with the pad. He was fearless.

At 1100, we went to Action Whitewater Adventures where we white water rafted down the South Fork of the American River. It was awesome! Melody and I had a blast. MD was uncertain with a scared look on his face the whole time. Andrew learned quickly how to white water raft and began guiding the trip together with our professional guide from Argentina. He could really read the current down the river and when to call out, "Forward, team!" meaning we had to paddle. After four hours we reached our destination and then loaded onto a bus and were driven back to the start. Once we processed our experience, we realized we all had a great time and would do it again.

Back at camp, we hung out. I went on my mountain bike and hit the trail around Camp Lotus. Andrew for the first time started our campfire with flint. He did it so fast, I didn't even get to see it. We were all proud of him. After dinner we hung out by the fire and made s'mores. It was a good time to hang out. Melody and MD slept in the tent, while Andrew and I slept in our hammocks.

The next morning, we packed up and drove to Lake Tahoe and camped at Meeks Bay! So awesome! We had an absolute blast! We played in the lake, rode our bikes around camp, played, and had fun. We had the most wonderful camp hosts, Rick and Michelle. Andrew wanted to make a campfire but we had no wood. He went over to their RV and asked so politely and Rick gave us some firewood for free to make s'mores.

The next day, Melody had to go into town for some work stuff for three hours. So, the boys and I hung out at the lake and rode our bikes around camp. When Melody came back, I took off and went mountain biking alone on the most amazing and breathtaking four-plus-mile trail. It was so much fun. Most of it was a wide trail then a single track. I was so thankful that we brought our mountain bikes. When I got back, I told Melody we had to ride it together as a family after dinner. We did just that. We got on our bikes after dinner and headed out. Now, Melody does not bike much and I knew this was going to be a challenge for her. At mile one, I realized that this ride might be too much for her, so I tried to suggest we turn back or at least Melody and Andrew (Andrew did not want to go riding) turn back and MD and I can ride the rest and meet up at camp. She never stopped. She persevered and was determined to finish the ride no matter how much her bottom, wrists, back, legs, etc hurt. She did this ride for the love of our family. I was truly proud of her and so thankful she stuck it out. It was an amazing mountain bike ride. She was still sore and bruised the next day.

It was bittersweet the next morning as we packed up. I wanted to stay there much longer and explore. God creates all things so beautifully. We left the majestic Lake Tahoe and headed to Reno which is very hot, dry, and less green with less pine trees. We drove to my friend Shelli's house. She and I went to nursing school together fourteen years ago, and both of us could not have gone through it without one another. I am so grateful for her. While we waited for her and her family to get off work, we drove around the city of Reno and made our way to a water park.

It was over 100 degrees and we needed to chill in the water and have some fun. Andrew hit the water rides right away, while MD timidly stood still in the middle of the park. Andrew wanted to go on another ride, so I went with him as an observer. Well, you see, this ride, you had to stand in a capsule and the foot platform dropped and so did you, down vertically on the slide. I told him I was not doing this. Andrew was fearless. He walked up, got on, and whoosh, there he went several stories vertically down. I raced down the stairs to congratulate him. He liked it except that he hit the back of his head on the slide. As Andrew and I stood at the bottom of the slide that he just went on, we could see that MD was still standing there, he had never moved. He must have been there for at least ten or fifteen minutes. Andrew, in an act of kindness, ran up to MD, grabbed his hand and encouraged him and took him on a ride. They rode ride after ride after that. Melody and I joined in on all the fun too. It was family time and making new memories.

After two and a half hours we caught up with Shelli and her husband, John. We went out for dinner and some ice cream. It had been a long time since we had seen each other. We caught up on each other's lives. She is now a Nurse Practitioner. She is an incredible woman, driven and so smart. I am so thankful she was my partner during nursing school. We have accomplished a lot as nurses and have come a long way. I am proud of what we have become in our nursing careers.

The next morning, we said our goodbyes and headed home, but stopped halfway due to the long nine-hour drive home. We slept in a hotel somewhere off Interstate 5, and the next morning drove home to drop MD off at a birthday party at 1230 at the beach where he then spent the night at his friend's house with six other soon-to-be junior high school boys. School started on Wednesday, so it was good for MD to spend his last summer days with his closest guy friends before he went into seventh grade at a new school.

I am so grateful for my family and to spend quality time with them on this road trip. I think it has made us more of a cohesive family. We learned teamwork and celebrated the gift of marriage. Our children experienced leadership, kindness, and taking risks. They reflected on the impact and value of friendships, personal perseverance, determination, and achievements. I saw the reflection of God's love for us in His beautiful creation, His protection, His guidance, and His grace.

Another Year at the Carpinteria Triathlon

September 30, 2018

Triathlon Season 2018 was coming to an end for my two boys. Their last race was the Carpinteria Sprint Triathlon. The boys started off in the same wave together on the swim, but MD within seconds was off with a perfect stroke propelling him further and further ahead, I never saw him again during the entire race. MD was so strong, even though he was sick with a cold toward the end of the week. His 500-meter swim was awesome, 21:04 compared to last year's 24:06. He flew on the 9-mile bike course, shaving 4 minutes off his time. He had stamina in his legs to carry him through the 3.1-mile run, holding the same time as last year. MD had knocked 14 minutes 25 seconds on his overall time from last year, which put him in podium position, receiving a second place in his age group division.

To ease the pounding hearts of worry from my wife and my mom, I agreed to be in the water with Andrew and swim next to him (which the race director let me do). Andrew entered the water with fear and chattering teeth from the cold water from the very start. It was a long, long battle to keep Andrew moving forward in the water for 500 meters. He cried for at least 35 minutes while he laid on his back and kicked. We stopped a few times to refocus, calm him down, and just hold him in my arms as other competitors passed us by. The lifeguards on their boards asked us if we needed help, but I said we were ok. At one point, I did call them over so Andrew could just rest on top of the board.

About halfway, Andrew wanted to quit and swim back to shore. We had this father-son moment when I shared with him, in my arms, how I have struggled with my job and want to quit, because it is so hard, at times so hard to breathe, like in the ocean. I told him that I am not quitting or giving up, but I am hanging in there and trying my best. I continued to encourage him as he kicked on his back. The final buoy was at our grasp and we made the turn into shore. We reached the beach in 43 minutes or so. This was even longer than last year's swim which was 32 minutes. I was worried that he would not have any leg power after kicking all that way without his use of his arms. He made it to transition, frustrated and exhausted. He slowly changed into his biking gear and headed off on the 9-mile bike course. He was on his own, however, I took my bike and made sure he was safe on the course.

For a good portion of the race, there was no bike lane and a very tight shoulder. He cruised on the bike course with a thumbs up. He pushed through the hills and pedaled his way down the final stretch, shaving 5 minutes off his last year's time. He made a very quick transition and was off on the run course, while I rode my bike encouraging along the way. His legs looked tired but he was determined to finish the race strong. He had an impressive 40:45 on the 3.1 mile run taking off 3 minutes 11 seconds from last year. He crossed the finish line in 2:23:58, placing second place in his age group division. He was able to shave 5 minutes of his overall race time, even with the long swim. He really gave it his all. I was so proud of his accomplishment.

It was wonderful to see both boys stand on the podium, medals around their necks, to see the smiles of success, and a sigh of relief that it is finished. Way to go boys. You did it!

It was a long day. The boys just chilled in their rooms, while I put away all the gear and bikes, because that is what dads do. I hope both boys compete in triathlons next year, but maybe Andrew might stand on the sidelines cheering his brother on as he shared with me during the run that he does not want to race next year. If only swimming pools were 500-meters long, he would do it in a heartbeat. He asked about considering doing a relay race so someone else could do the swim. It is good to see him want to still compete, just not so much in the ocean.

I learned a lot about patience and perseverance during this race. It reminds me of how God is so patient with us and does not leave our side when we are struggling, crying, and want to throw in the towel. One of the things I have gone over and over and tried to teach and coach Andrew is to freestyle when he swims in the ocean and not just doggie paddle/vertical swim. When he races, he has his own way and I try to tell him his way makes you more tired and does not propel you in a forward motion. God, in His Word, helps coach us along our path in our faith. We—I—know I try to doggie paddle my way through my faith and it is hard. I hope Andrew and I learn how to listen to our Father who knows what is best for us and act upon it.

Just Me & God - Winter Sierra Trip

January 18-21, 2019

The past year has been a very emotional, psychological, physical, and spiritual road for me as I face a difficult challenge in my work. I never thought I would be in this situation in my nursing career, but this is where God has me as I am learning to trust Him in the storm. I can relate to the disciples of Jesus in Matthew 8:23-27: Then he got into the boat and his disciples followed him. Suddenly a furious storm came up on the lake, so that the waves swept over the boat. But Jesus was sleeping. The disciples went and woke him, saying, "Lord, save us! We're going to drown!" He replied, "You of little faith, why are you so afraid?" Then he got up and rebuked the winds and the waves, and it was completely calm. The men were amazed and asked, "What kind of man is this? Even the winds and the waves obey him!" In the midst of this storm, I have seen the blessings of God and I am learning to be still and wait on Him as He strengthens my heart to have great courage.

During a recent visit to my doctor, the question was asked if I am exercising. My wife, Melody, at my side at the doctor's visit, says, "No, not for the past three to five months." So, instead of going for a walk on the beach, I left for the Western Sierras alone. I left Friday afternoon and headed to Visalia to stay the night at my friend Ryan's house with his family. It is a five-hour drive to the Sierras, so I split it up. The next morning, I left at 0530 and drove to the Huntington Lake area and delivered my homemade brownies (that I made from scratch since we now have an oven and new kitchen) to Daryl at the Tamarack Lodge and to Mayor Mark. Mayor Mark offered to take me by snowmobile to my location, around 5.5 miles or so. So, I waited for two hours until he was ready to take me. He had some friends with him. As I waited near my car with my gear, he showed up and said, "Here you go! I am heading off with my buddies on snowmobiles, so here is your snowmobile and have fun and bring it back when you are done." I thought he was joking, until he walked away while the snowmobile was running.

I only drove one for my first time last year and that was an eye opener. So, I loaded my gear onto his sled behind the snowmobile. It took me twenty-five minutes to get it running. No one was around to help me or tell me if I am doing it wrong. I finally headed off up the mountain trail. I made it safely to my destination, which was the spot where Smiley Andy and I went last winter with the big ski hill. It was a quick twenty minutes, much faster than alpine skiing pulling a pulk sled behind me. It was a blast! I parked it underneath some trees and put a tarp over it as a roof-like covering because a storm was coming the next day. I was really nervous about taking care of Mayor Mark's snowmobile.

Then I made camp. I set up my Kammok hammock, kitchen area, dining area, and an area for my gear. As I laid in my hammock, I heard cracks coming from one of my anchor points, which was an old dead tree that seemed solid at the time. Nope, it was not. A few pushes on the tree and it tipped over. I am so thankful that it did not fall over in the middle of the night while I was sleeping in my hammock. So, I had to rebuild my living situation. As I was finishing up, Mayor Mark and his friends came by to check on me and to see if I made it safely by snowmobile. We said our goodbyes and he said, "I will see you in a few days." Then an hour later, a guy named Chris who was alpine touring next to my campsite came over and told me that he comes up here frequently. We chatted for a while and exchanged numbers. He always does this alone and would love to have someone go with him. I told him I would love that. It was great to connect with him.

I collected wood for a fire for the next two days and dragged that dead tree over to my fire pit with the use of my pulk sled. Then I went downhill skiing, just a minute away from where I set up camp, just the way I wanted to. It was so much fun. Then when I got to the bottom, I put on my skins underneath my skis and climbed back up the hill. Once I got back, I made dinner with my REI purchase of dehydrated Chicken Pad Thai next to the fire. It was okay. Not like what you get in Thailand where my dad lives. Then I snuggled into my sleeping bag inside my Kammok hammock and read my Bible and prayed. It was great. I slept okay. I got up a few times, had a headache and was thirsty. The elevation was 8,000+ feet. I decided, since I was up, to cut down a dead tree to use for the next day, this was around 2400 hours. I never really do sleep when I camp. There are so many things that are new and different. I am so used to the sound of my wife's Hepa filter in our room or that pillow I love. Also, the nuances of being in a beautiful place and where there are bears and other large animals that like eating meat. I am always on my guard.

Morning finally arrived and I made breakfast and then made a trek by skis towards West Lake, 3.5 miles round trip. I was close to West Lake and could see Red Mountain in the distance just behind West Lake but it was time to head back, it looked stormy. When I got back, I ate my dehydrated Chicken Fettuccine Alfredo for lunch which filled me up all day and I did not even eat dinner. I had also set up my tent just in case I needed it during the storm. I am so thankful I did. The storm came in hard leaving its trace in the area where my living area was underneath the tarp. It was completely covered in snow. I had taken my hammock down just before the storm hit. All night, the wind and snow hit my tent. I thought, if I climbed out of my tent, the wind would just blow it away even with the bomber anchors I had in place. For a brief moment, the storm ceased and I got out and it had dumped over a foot of snow. It was so quiet after listening to the storm, such a contrast from the past five hours. I climbed back into my tent and within a minute or two, the storm was back, dumping another foot of snow.

By morning, it was so white and quiet. My old foot tracks were gone and I was creating new ones. I ate breakfast and packed up my gear. Before I left, I took advantage of the new soft snow on the hill below me. I put on my skis and headed down the slope making effort-less turns down the feather-like snow, soft and fluffy. It was awesome, incredible, amazing, and so peaceful. I wanted to do this over and over, but there are no chair lifts here. I was tired by the time I got back up the hill with my skins and skis on.

I took off my skis and said goodbye to this place. I loaded the gear onto the sled behind the snowmobile. It took me fifteen or twenty minutes to start the snowmobile. There was a small knob to pull up on, that was the on and off switch, which I figured out after ten minutes went by. I was still learning the instrument panel of this massive beast they call a snowmobile. As I started to move, it got stuck in the deep snow. I spent another ten or fifteen minutes digging the snow out from underneath the snowmobile and in front of it. I finally got it going down the hill and ran into a pickle at the bottom.

There were trees blocking my way to the main trail. I had of course stopped which then caused the snowmobile to get stuck in the deep powder snow. I dug it out again. To my left, I noticed a gap between two trees about four feet apart. I thought this was my only option and Mayor Mark might not be looking for me until tomorrow or something like that. As I went by the two trees, I was on the left of the snowmobile to put more weight on the hill side. As I did this, my body struck the branches of the tree on the left and knocked me off into the tree well. The snowmobile was at shoulder height now. I was covered in snow and wondering how I was going to get out of this pickle. I put my climbing experience into practice. I managed to climb up and over the snowmobile, start the machine and continued on reaching the main trail. I cruised all the way back to my destination until I had to go up a steep short trail to the main road. I overshot the turn and got stuck. I again dug the snowmobile out and lifted it so that it was in line with the hill. After another twenty minutes, I jumped and shook the snowmobile and got it up the hill and onto the road and parked it next to my car.

I unloaded my gear and put it into the car. My car was buried with snow, because the snow plow pushed a wall of snow along my car. It was stuck. Mayor Mark showed up and congratulated me for returning back safely, but now he had to tow my car out the snow. I am so grateful for him. We laughed about my stories and adventures of the weekend and said our goodbyes. I left for home with a huge pile of snow on top of the roof lasting for at least two hours. I arrived safely at home.

I am deeply grateful for this weekend and having mostly alone time. I had the opportunity to spend time with God, meditate on Him, and seek His wisdom and direction for my life. I experienced His protection from the elements, His safety, joy through His creation, and many blessings that came from Him. I am constantly reminded of the words of Psalms 27:14, that says, "Wait on the LORD. Be of good courage, and He will strengthen your heart. Wait, I say, on the LORD."

A Day at China Peak with the Boys - Winter Sierra Trip

March 24-27, 2019

MD, Smiley Andy and I hit the Western Sierras for four days this past weekend. We drove up after church on Sunday. We delivered our traditional cookies and brownies, made by Melody, to our friends Mayor Mark, Daryl, and for some staff at China Peak Lodge. We ate dinner in our room, relaxed, and went to sleep. In the morning, we started out at China Peak Lodge and skied the bunny slopes, which was a first for all of us. This was MD's first time downhill skiing which was a struggle. He lasted about two and a half hours and was done. He went to eat lunch and then went to the car to hang out. That did not stop Andrew and I. We skied for another hour and a half. He shredded the slopes, fearless, even trying a harder slope.

At 1300, Monday afternoon, we got in our car and drove to the start of Tamarack Trail and from there we skied while I pulled a pulk sled to our base camp which was so beautiful. This was a spot where MD and I had camped years ago. We had the Tamarack Creek flowing next to us. Tons of snow. I set up camp and made our cozy kitchen/dining/living room area with pine branches to sit on and keep our feet off the snow while the kids were asleep in the tent for an hour and a half. These boys were tired. MD came out of the tent first and said, "Wow! Taking a nap feels so good and now I have lots of energy." He then was on a mission to collect firewood. For dinner we had our traditional tri-tip over the fire, so yummy. Everybody went to bed early.

The next day, we had eggs and sausage and played around camp. Andrew and I went and explored the creek on our touring skis. It was so much fun. The boys dug small snow caves, had snowball fights, collected more wood, and played games like Scrabble in the tent. Since it was a beautiful day, I got in the water and even floated on my Nemo pad. Yes, it was really cold, but I had to try it out. Bear Grylls would have been proud. I had some great quality time with God on the serene bank of the creek. Later I went up to the top of a ridge to get cell reception to check in with Melody, I love her. Evening came around, and we ate spaghetti. It did not taste all that great. "Too much sauce", according to Andrew. The boys went to bed early. I stayed up and collected more firewood. I also ran out of fuel for the stove. My stove was clogging and had some issues. I was worried about breakfast the next morning. The kids wanted pancakes and hot chocolate and I had to deliver.

I got up in the morning and built a fire and was able to cook right over it, watching carefully as the pot balanced on several logs. Breakfast was delicious. After we were done eating, a storm started creeping in. It started snowing and MD said, "We better pack up quickly." So, we did. Snow was coming down hard at least 8 inches during the hour and a half while we were packing inside the tent. When we were ready to break down the tent, the snowing ceased as we loaded all the gear on the pulk sled. It remained clear skies until we reached our car, but then the snow came back hard. We made it back home around 1900 after our usual In-N-Out stop and as usual, I take everything out of the car and unpack by myself. But this time, Andrew came into the garage and asked several times, "What can I do to help." Both boys helped for a while, Melody brought dinner home from the Chicken Ranch, and then we got ready for bed.

It was a fun trip! It was wonderful to see MD learn how to downhill ski even though it was challenging for him. He might want to do it again later in life. I loved bonding with my sons. It was definitely needed. Between the kids going to school, school work, baseball practices and games, we have not had time to just spend good quality time together. They are amazing kids.

Take Me Out to the Ball Game

2019

Let's play baseball! This year MD and Smiley Andy both wanted to play baseball. This was MD's second year playing but now in the Juniors Division (the big leagues before high school baseball). He grew so much and his confidence and skills improved leaps and bounds. He can really smack that baseball with confidence even after being hit in the wrist by a pitched ball twice this season and twice last season. He is never afraid of the pitchers who throw almost 90 miles an hour. He is one tough kid. I am so proud of his accomplishments. I love watching him bat. However, I was so nervous and could not sit still or be quiet in the bleachers. I paced back and forth, so excited for him. He enjoys playing outfielder and is getting really good at it. His team is currently first place in his division and playoffs start this next week.

This season was Smiley Andy's first year playing baseball in the Minors Division. You would not know it by the end of the season. I was able to be one of the coaches which was a true blessing and joy. He loves this sport and is really great at it. He is a strong outfielder, second baseman, and third baseman. He is willing to play any position his coach makes him play. He gives 110% all the time. Although his team lost every game he had a wonderful and joyful attitude. He loved talking with the other team players while playing infield. He encouraged his teammates. He made sure everyone knew where to throw the ball to get the next person out, "Play at first and second and watch the steal!" He made some great slides into home plate scoring runs for the team. He made a double hit at bat as well. He loved stealing bases. His favorite moments were getting to pitch in two games towards the end of the season and then the final inning in the last playoff game. He never was nervous. He would always look at me while he was standing at the pitching mound to receive encouragement and give me a look that said, "I've got this, Dad." I rarely sat in the stands as I cheered for him when he made another great play, catch, throw, or swing. He hustled around the bases while you could hear his dad if you were a mile away, "RUN Andrew, RUN! SLIDE Andrew, SLIDE!"

Although I love taking my kids on adventures in the mountains, I really embraced the moments while they were on the field. It was an adventure for sure. I enjoyed coaching with Andrew's baseball team and practicing in the backyard with my sons to build on their skills. They are so precious and I love being their dad. I am their biggest fan and everyone knew it especially in the bleachers, the dugout, and on the field. They are winners in my book!

Last Remaining Thoughts

Thank you for reading my "novel." It has been a blessing to share with you the adventures, the challenges, the joys and celebrations, the growth of my children and my growth as a father. I hope this has inspired you, encouraged you, challenged you, and motivated you to become the best father or role model that you can be. It is a lifelong journey that makes the greatest impact on our children's lives. Stay tuned for more adventures yet to come…

Thank you again to my most wonderful and beautiful wife, Melody. I love you. You have brought these two beautiful boys into our lives. Thank you for always entrusting our children to me on these adventures. Thank you for your love, support, encouragement, and your help.

MD and Smiley Andy, I love you so much. You are so precious. I believe in you. I am proud of you. I will always be there for you. You are strong. You are courageous. You make an impact in people's lives. I pray and hope that you will someday pass on the things that your mom and I have taught you and the experiences that you have gained through your adventures with me, with your own family, sons and daughters someday. I love you with all my heart.

Made in the USA
San Bernardino, CA
14 August 2020